Smallx20:
Twenty Years of Community-Engaged Design in New Orleans

I0869631

APPLIED
RESEARCH
+DESIGN

Published by Applied Research and Design Publishing, an imprint of ORO Editions.
Gordon Goff: Publisher

www.appliedresearchanddesign.com
info@appliedresearchanddesign.com

Authors: Maggie Hansen, Nick Jenisch, Ann Yoachim, Emilie Taylor Welty
Book Design: Jose Cotto, Nick Jenisch, Amy Martin
Project Manager: Jake Anderson
Cover Photo: David Armentor

10 9 8 7 6 5 4 3 2 1 First Edition

ISBN: 978-1-966515-09-8

Prepress and Print work by ORO Editions Inc.

Printed in China

AR+D Publishing makes a continuous effort to minimize the overall carbon footprint of its publications. As part of this goal, AR+D, in association with Global ReLeaf, arranges to plant trees to replace those used in the manufacturing of the paper produced for its books. Global ReLeaf is an international campaign run by American Forests, one of the world's oldest nonprofit conservation organizations. Global ReLeaf is American Forests' education and action program that helps individuals, organizations, agencies, and corporations improve the local and global environment by planting and caring for trees.

Smallx20: Twenty Years of Community-Engaged Design in New Orleans

Maggie Hansen
Nick Jenisch
Ann Yoachim
Emilie Taylor Welty

Introduction
Anna Livia Brand

Guest Contributors
Austin Allen, Scott Bernhard, Jackson Blalock, Pam Broom, Maxwell Ciardullo, Maurice Cox, Dan Etheridge, Rashida Ferdinand, Johanna Gilligan, Anya Groner, Doug Harmon, Bahareh Javadi, Melissa Lee, Jazmin Miller, Suzanne-Juliette Mobley, Andreanecia Morris, Sarah Satterlee, jackie sumell, Matt Williams

Additional Text
Jose Cotto, Suzanne-Juliette Mobley

Graphic Design
Jose Cotto, Nick Jenisch, Amy Martin

Editing
Amy Lenkiewicz

Table of Contents

Small Steps to Radical Futures

Making and Dreaming Together

The Albert and Tina Small Center for Collaborative Design has been shaped by large forces: the creative cultures of New Orleans, the subtropical and low-lying environment of the Mississippi Delta, and the failed governmental response to a catastrophic storm. However, a force just as important to the Center's work has been small-scale: the desire of individual community members to collaborate in building a better city. Like other organizations formed in the wake of Hurricane Katrina, the Center's founders applied ad hoc and responsive methods of work to address the immediate needs of New Orleans communities. Unlike other design initiatives founded and shaped by a singular charismatic leader, Small Center was established by the input of many voices and the work of many hands—an ethos that continues to inform the Center's work twenty years later.

Some credit its origin to a vocal group of students and faculty who wanted their work in school to have an impact outside campus. Others credit administrators who saw the value in service learning and secured the funding to adapt this model to New Orleans. Both stories are true, and the Center's origin lies in the right people joining together in a way particular to New Orleans, a city shaped by creativity and tenacity. The Center's collaborative origin is symbolic of the values upon which it operates today: design practice characterized by shared leadership, a broad definition of architectural skills, and a commitment to community input.

The very establishment of the Center can be considered the Center's first "design" project. It is fitting that multiple people are credited with the idea, and that there was no singular figurehead, since co-authorship is at the core of the Center's approach. From the start, each person's contribution was valued and recognized for moving the work forward. This is rare in design and in academia, where there is pressure to claim authorship of products and ownership of ideas, even though projects are realized through teamwork. Collaboration and shared leadership have been a characteristic of the Center from the start and continue to be so today.

The Center has had five directors and has benefitted from the support of four deans of the Tulane School of Architecture and Built Environment. The Center's staff has included nationally recognized and emerging leaders in architecture and allied disciplines. Each project has been developed in dialogue with local community groups and characterized by deep, strategic engagement processes. The Center's work arises from the context, the people, and the conversations of the moment, but looks towards the future. As part of an academic institution, the Center trains the next generation of design leaders in the tools of community engaged practice.

Though models of social practice in design education can be traced back to the 1930s, community design centers first emerged in the 1960s, informed by civil rights activism.[1] In the 1990s and 2000s, the number of these design programs centers surged to meet the needs of communities traditionally underserved by the design disciplines. Among them, Auburn University's Rural Studio, established in 1993 in Hale County, Alabama, demonstrated a model in which architecture students brought their energy and skills to design and construct homes for residents of an underserved, rural community. Inspired by the growing discourse around design in the public interest, a coalition of faculty and students at Tulane imagined a similar opportunity at their school, in which students gained hands-on experience while working in service to real clients, meeting tangible needs in the New Orleans community.

Small Center leadership traces the Center's formation to Reed Kroloff, dean of the School of Architecture in 2005, who brought to Tulane his own interest in service learning. Founding Assistant Director Dan Etheridge was working at the Tulane/Xavier Center for Bioenvironmental Research when he heard Dean Kroloff speak at a university luncheon about developing a program in which students' coursework could contribute to addressing community needs. Inspired, he talked with Kroloff about how he might use his talents for relationship-building and grant writing to realize the project. Urbanist and Associate Dean Ila Berman refined the scope of the program, aspiring to develop prototypes of urban design and affordable housing across the city as tangible models for other urban contexts. Her proposal to HUD, matched with donor funding, set the financial foundation for the Center's first projects.

For almost two decades, Small Center has sought to realize design's potential to contribute to social change. Its designers have imagined, constructed, and advocated for spaces that sustain, heal, and foster community well-being. The Center works at a range of scales, from projects as small as bicycle carts to those as large as planning programs revitalizing historic commercial corridors. No matter the size, deep engagement shapes each project, so that the Center's work embodies the belief that all residents are impacted by the built environment and should have the right to meaningfully participate in the decisions that shape it.

Centering Collaboration

New Orleans is a city where life is celebrated, negotiated, and expressed in the claiming and use of public space. Much of Small Center's work, built on public land or for public use, takes part in this conversation.

The Center primarily participates by listening to the needs of nonprofits and community groups. Small Center's projects are not initiated by the Center or by individual faculty interests. Rather, the Center lends its expertise, energy, and influence to amplify existing efforts. Design work takes time, as does collaboration. Local nonprofits are willing to invest the time to collaborate with the Center because the Center has attained a level of community embeddedness beyond that of a typical design studio. By prioritizing local relationship-building, accountability has come to include project conversations at the grocery store or in line to vote. The Center has also become known through the physical footprint it has made on the built environment of the city. Its work is about bringing people together who have geography in common and finding they may have other things in common, too.

Ultimately, the Center's working style is a process of relationship-building, including across disciplines. Transdisciplinary work is characterized by appropriate–but disparate–expertise, gathered to tackle a specific problem. Exchanging rules, procedures, and definitions, collaborators form a new set of terms, common to the group, unique to the task at hand,

and shaped by the translation across disparate expertise and approaches. By bringing in many voices, these collaborations decenter the designer, ensuring that the visual language that emerges across the body of the Center's work is multivocal: each project's aesthetic speaking to the tastes of each partner organization.

At times, the Center's work has been critiqued for not having a signature architecture style. However, to have such a style would mean the Center imposing its own vision upon community spaces. Instead, the Center is a chameleon by design. Its design process aims to engage extensively with the community to yield a highly tailored product. Each project's aesthetic language, interim goals, and final development is decided through ongoing dialogue across the design team, the partner organization's leadership and staff, local stakeholders, possible funders, and other strategic experts and allies. This approach results in a body of dissimilar work, that has earned Small Center recognition as a national leader in community-based design and can be traced back to its founding.

Ad Hoc, Experimental, Nimble, Responsive Practices

In 2005, the idea for a public interest design program at Tulane gained enough traction that the Albert and Tina Small Center for Collaborative Design (then the Tulane City Center) was established. Its role was to act as the outreach arm of the Tulane School of Architecture. From the start, the Center was imagined as a transdisciplinary endeavor, its founding mission to bring "a design-driven, environmentally responsible, and socially conscious urban design agenda to New Orleans." In the months leading up to Hurricane Katrina, and in collaboration with the Tulane/ Xavier Center for Bioenvironmental Research, the Center was charged with identifying potential projects and pursuing the funding to support them. The Center's first partnership was with the local nonprofit, Neighborhood Housing Services of New Orleans (NHSNO). NHSNO tasked the Center with designing and building a series of single-family, affordable housing prototypes in Central City neighborhoods suffering from disinvestment. The first prototype, a 1400-square-foot house in Central City, was designed in the summer of 2005, with construction set to take place in the Fall semester. The studio instructor, Doug Harmon, and one of the student participants, Emilie Taylor, were vocal proponents of the program and became key figures in shaping its trajectory.

The Holy Ghost House prototype was never realized. The studio class was preparing to break ground on August 29, 2005. That morning, Hurricane Katrina made landfall just east of New Orleans. Though the eye of the storm missed the city, the damage was catastrophic. Failures in the city's system of floodwalls and levees resulted in a foot or more of flood water in eighty percent of the city and damage to at least every three out of four homes.

In Louisiana, the storm took an estimated 1,500 lives. Millions of residents were left homeless, and cultural spaces, businesses, neighborhood anchors, and family heirlooms were damaged or destroyed. Failures at the local, state, and federal levels compounded in a chaotic disaster response. Historic patterns of city development, based on race and class, left poor and working-class Black residents most vulnerable to flooding. The funding to rebuild was inequitably distributed based on the pre-storm value of housing, which was lower in those same neighborhoods, magnifying existing injustices.

The City was burdened by immediate needs and ended up prioritizing new investment and tourism. Initial redevelopment plans proposed to reshape the city geographically and demographically, while returning residents dealt with their own immediate needs, trauma, and the difficulty of returning to a decimated city. However, a grassroots resistance to this top-down reshaping of the city developed, perhaps beginning with reactions against the infamous redevelopment proposal known as the "Green Dot Plan."[2] In the face of possible erasure, residents came together to create their own recovery plans and advocate for the needs of the hardest hit neighborhoods.

2005 - 2008

The Center's early work coordinated grassroots recovery efforts with those of peer institutions that came to New Orleans to assist. During the Fall of 2005, Tulane students and faculty spent an evacuation semester on the Arizona State University campus. Back in New Orleans, conversations about the city's recovery prioritized input from political leaders and outside experts. Residents had few opportunities to share their needs and concerns.

To begin to amplify the voices of community members, co-hosts Tulane, Loyola, and Xavier Universities convened *Reinhabiting New Orleans*. Organized by Small Center, the event brought together national advocacy organizations and technical experts in finance, architecture, and planning, with leaders of community organizations, artists, creatives, and residents who had been engaged in their neighborhoods before the storm. Notably, the event paid for displaced residents' attendance-related expenses, allowing representatives from some of the hardest-hit communities to attend. Residents' short- and long-term needs, as reported by neighborhood leaders in the meeting, informed the first eighteen months of the Center's work. The two-day convening centered around facilitated discussions, story circles, and neighborhood tours that highlighted the lived and embodied knowledge of the city, while putting these narratives in dialogue with technical experts. This format also set an important precedent for the Center to act as an ally in amplifying community-led initiatives.

One month later, the Center participated in a follow-up conference at the University of Arkansas in which university design programs from across the country came together to identify ways to contribute to the rebuilding effort. Initially ten schools committed to work together to address immediate and long-term needs in the city. These schools formed the CITYbuild Consortium. Small Center, with support from Design Corps, served as the matchmaker between university programs and New Orleans nonprofits, facilitating their collaborations. By December 2006, CITYbuild included contributions from thirty national and international design programs, in partnership with twenty local organizations. Sixteen structures were built or rehabilitated and over 200 proposals were developed to visualize community needs. The program demonstrated a model of intra-university partnership in response to disaster and was recognized with the ACSA's 2007-08 Collaborative Practice Award. CITYbuild laid the foundation for the Center's commitment to collaborating with other community design centers.

Funding from private donors and national organizations supported these early efforts. While CITYbuild put the Center in dialogue with national leaders in public interest design, local efforts established a reputation for trust and responsiveness in New Orleans. The studio model developed for the Holy Ghost House was adapted to create the URBANbuild program, which prototyped affordable housing informed by the local context.[3] Tulane students worked collectively to design, develop, and build these prototypes, bringing the unique vernacular architecture of New Orleans housing into a contemporary design language. The first four URBANbuild prototypes were designed and constructed as projects of the Center, with support from private donors, Tulane University, and a Gulf Coast Assistance grant from the Department of Housing and Urban Development. In 2010, URBANbuild separated from the Center to become a separate initiative. Today, it continues this model of university-based design-build in coordination with local housing nonprofits.

After *Reinhabiting New Orleans*, the Center saw more clearly the costs and benefits of organizations from across the country flocking to New Orleans to lend a hand. This influx of outside assistance created impromptu partnerships and brought access to additional resources, but it also compartmentalized relief efforts and inhibited expeditious planning. As early as December 2006, social justice organizers drafted an open letter to foundations and funders describing their frustrations:

> Instead of prioritizing efforts led by people who are from the communities most affected, we have seen millions of dollars [...] either remain unspent or shuttled to well-placed outsiders with[,] at best, a cursory knowledge of the realities faced by people here. Instead of reflecting local needs and priorities, many projects funded reflect outside perception of what our priorities should be.[4]

Many of the signatories of the open letter became Small Center partners.

The Center remained responsive to local needs through different phases of disaster recovery, from frantic rebuilding to the relative stability post-recovery stability. The Center formalized the role it played in post-Katrina efforts, connecting organizations to resources, by developing a Request for Proposals (RFP) process. Project selection was formalized and included a jury process that included past partners, community leaders, students, and university representatives. Projects were evaluated for need and potential impact. In implementing the chosen projects, Small Center ensured a deep engagement process and high-quality design. A corporate gift from Johnson Controls committed to funding across ten-years, allowing the Center to establish the RFP as an annual opportunity. The Center also participated in funders' forums, advised funders, and navigated its own identity in the complex post-disaster philanthropic landscape, where rapidly shifting local needs and funding priorities were often out of alignment.

2008 - 2014

By conducting multiple projects within specific neighborhoods, the Center identified and advanced synergies. By 2010, the Center had completed over fifty projects at a range of scales by focusing the majority of its work in a topographic zone above the extent of Katrina-related flooding but below sea-level. The projects represented community visions of how low-lying land might be valuable in new ways as spaces for recreation, urban agriculture, soil remediation, or stormwater management.[5] These projects filled a critical gap in the conversation about rebuilding New Orleans with greater density on higher ground, illustrating the economic potential of alternative land uses for low-lying areas. The Center sought projects that would prototype these opportunities.

As project themes emerged, the Center connected with other organizations to share skills, networks, and support. These synergies resulted in multiple urban farming projects aimed at addressing food deserts across the city, as well as the co-location of projects in key areas of particular neighborhoods. Small Center worked on a number of projects in New Orleans' Lower and Upper Ninth Wards, assisting in both cultural preservation and climate resilience. Concurrent projects in Central City aimed to boost and reanimate existing cultural assets like the Mardi Gras Indian Council and the Dew Drop Inn to effect wider recognition of a proposed "Cultural Corridor." The Center developed a working relationship with City Park, a centrally accessible location, which became the home for multiple nonprofits serving local youth. For these efforts, the Center received local and national awards for its design and engagement processes, while the wider university garnered recognition for its commitment to New Orleans's recovery.

2014 - 2018

Significantly expanding its capacity and scope, Small Center moved off-campus into a building newly renovated to its specifications and centrally located for ease of access. The building provided on-site construction and prototyping space, classrooms for Tulane architecture design studios and seminars, and a "community storefront" space for hosting partners and curating exhibits. Multi-year funding from the Surdna Foundation supported a staff position dedicated to curating public programming and developing community engagement in the new space. The new building amplified projects' impact by presenting research associated with each project in a series of events and exhibits focused on the major issues facing New Orleans, expanding projects' relevance to a wider audience.

The Center also increased its full-time staff, hiring from a variety of disciplines, from landscape architecture to anthropology to planning. Enlarging its team allowed the Center to test new project types, including graphic advocacy campaigns with partners advocating for causes such as musicians' rights, the reduction of lead in water, climate resilience, and fair housing. Expanding its footprint through networking, publications, and national conferences, Small Center joined growing national conversations around public interest design. The Center also co-founded the Design Futures Student Leadership Forum, hosting national leaders and a cohort of students from across the country for a week of workshops and conversations about how design practice can better serve social justice. In 2016, the Center was renamed to recognize the generous support of Sonny and Tina Small. This naming gift allowed the Center to deepen its commitment to local communities and consider long-term goals for its work.

During this time, as population growth continued in post-recovery New Orleans, the Center was sensitive to rising housing costs and gentrification. In response, the Center ensured that projects overlapped with public programming, and that what was made privately available to some was also transparently visible by all. The end of this period, marked by the tenth anniversary of Hurricane Katrina, looked to shift city-wide focus beyond recovery and resilience towards a vibrant future.

2018 – Present

Small Center navigated a changing political climate and public health crisis, both of which impacted the Center's work. Covid-19 posed a serious challenge to deep, in-person community engagement. However, Tulane University and Small Center remained open and active, adapting with new outreach and teaching methods. National protests following the killing of George Floyd inspired critical reflection on how to address systemic racism in the built environment. Small Center engaged in national and local conversations in the months that followed and embraced new models of action alongside partners working in cultural and social justice spaces. Small Center continued expanding. It hired more staff with diverse academic backgrounds, including public health, arts education, and graphic design. It combined with the previously independent Tulane Regional Urban Design Center, adding planning-scale services to the design work offered in Small Center's Request for Proposals. It expanded its impact beyond New Orleans, partnering with Louisiana and Gulf South cities and mayors. By working with geographic breadth, the Center gained an understanding of the wider, regional context of its work in Orleans Parish. Its public programming evolved to include local artists, displaying their work in dialogue with that of nonprofit partners and academic researchers. These collaborations explored complex issues, from water management to inequitable zoning policy to criminal justice reform, all from multiple perspectives.

Alongside these efforts, the Center paused to critically reflect on its own past, hiring an outside assessment expert to conduct a full review of Small Center projects and partners. The outside assessment expert conducted interviews and site visits for fifty projects, representing fifteen years of Small Center history, from 2006-2020. Selected projects reflected a variety of work (from design-builds to exhibits), different sizes and scales, and a range of perceived successes and failures. Qualitative, in-person and online interviews with staff, faculty, and community partners ensured that projects were evaluated from various points of view.

The outcome of the assessment determined that some of the most valued parts of Small Center's work were aspects of the design and engagement process that went beyond a final building or graphic product. Partners valued the opportunity to build organizational capacity through their ongoing relationship with the Center's staff and its programming. This book is structured in response to what partners and participants valued most about our work, according to the impact evaluation. As public interest design education evolves, questions of inequity and design access evolve too, and impact evaluations, like the Center's, become pivotal.

Grounded in Place, Guided by Relationships

The Center's work is informed by, responsive to, and contingent upon, the City of New Orleans. In the two decades since Hurricane Katrina, through different stages of recovery and change, the Center's programs have adapted to fill emerging gaps and meet new challenges. Over the course of 160 projects, this work has established the Center as a national leader in public interest design.

Though Small Center's projects are grounded in specific local concerns, each project also grapples with the systemic issues that other U.S. cities face. The Center's working methods are appropriate for other community design initiatives operating within universities, balancing the instructional needs of design students with the practical needs of the communities served by each project. The Center offers a model for on-the-ground architectural research, as design faculty continue to face questions about what counts as research and how architectural products contribute to advancing new, scholarly knowledge–even as participatory action research and service-learning have gained traction.

This book explores Small Center's strategies for balancing these different (and at times conflicting) needs. As a means of sharing the Center's work and process, this book attempts to illustrate the complexity and the joyfulness of working in a manner that is open to the input of many different voices and perspectives.

Following this introduction, the essay "Holy Ghost Houses: Freedom as Location, Scale, and Tempo" reflects on New Orleans as a place that is made and remade through the humble and ongoing work of everyday residents in dialogue with the dynamics of their environment. Anna Livia Brand's work in New Orleans as a historian and a community-engaged planning scholar informs her reading of the local culture of activism and mutual aid that characterizes the city. The essay grounds the projects that follow in the planning and organizing culture that has influenced the Center's working methods.

Informed by the survey responses and staff reflections collected during the Center's impact assessment, the following chapters are organized according to the Center's six core, guiding principles. To illustrate how these core principles have been refined through experimentation, reflection, and changes in the city, project narratives are introduced chronologically within each chapter. These analytical and visual essays show how the Center has applied architectural skills to address different community needs.

To complement and complicate Small Center's own narrative, we have invited key participants to reflect on Small Center's identity at crucial stages in its history. These guest reflections include writings by leaders of partner organizations, designers, former students, and previous staff members. The reflections offer personal accounts of the work, the people, and the place at different moments in the Center's life. Each chapter illustrates the Center's distinct responses to each project's needs and the many ways it advances social change.

The first two chapters situate the Center's work within the larger conversation New Orleans communities are holding, outside of the Center, to define their own needs. From the start, the Center has recognized the necessity of holding space for neighborhood leaders and community groups to engage in the big conversations about the city's future. Every resident is impacted by the built environment and should have a voice in shaping it.

The first chapter, "Gathering with Communities," demonstrates the role of exhibits, special events, and open gatherings as critical to shaping the city, since these meetings support conversations that discuss the future of the built environment. The projects in this chapter illustrate how holding space for joy, food, and fellowship builds personal connections that later become alliances for lasting social change.

The Center has gathered community in different ways, each permutation shaping design projects and city policy distinctly. In 2014, the Center intentionally used its "storefront" as a test site for different types of events. The different events led to different conversations, shaping the Center's project priorities, approaches, and partnerships accordingly. Gathering is key to how projects come to Small Center, so drawing different people into the room meant that Small Center's projects shifted responsively. Even the Center's annual Request for Proposals evaluation is a kind of conversation, as local leaders with diverse perspectives review proposals from New Orleans-based nonprofits through discussion. The stories we tell when we gather inform our imagination about the future and its possibilities.

The second chapter, "Recovering Stories of Place," reflects on the role of narrative in shaping collective ideas of the city. By giving a platform to collective storytelling, Small Center elevates the expertise of lived experience and highlights the value of cultural traditions, not just the spaces that hold them. Narrative and visual stories are essential tools for the Center to bring human experience to policy discussions.

As a university-based design program, the Center is responsible for educating emerging design leaders while navigating town and gown. Students who participate in Small Center's work are exposed to an approach to design and learning that is deeply connected to life in New Orleans. Through coursework, lectures, workshops, and fellowships, the Center demonstrates the value of an expanded set of architectural tools. Students gain experience working with clients on real projects and see the significance of their skills in contributing to change. The Center's work illustrates that designing and constructing buildings can be a meaningful step in improving life for community members, as well as showing that architects can contribute in many ways beyond making buildings.

Chapter 3, "Making, Doing, Testing," explores the skills that designers can bring to social practice and methods of learning through creative production. The projects in this chapter illustrate how the Center balances student design education with community-based work. The chapter explains how the Center teaches students the importance of learning the context, history, and culture of project neighborhoods and sites. It also explores how studio-based education, and the skill of thinking-by-making shape the creative engagement practices of Small Center students and faculty.

The fourth chapter, "Amplifying Knowledge on the Ground," demonstrates how tools of architectural practice can be used for advocacy. Projects in this chapter demonstrate the limitations of relying on data and design alone. Instead, projects here elevate the status of lived experience to an essential part of understanding place and context. To lead a collaborative process towards effective design proposals, the Center teaches students how to spend time listening, asking questions, and getting to know the everyday rhythms of the communities they engage. This teaching strategy responds to students' desire to use their creativity and skills for social change. The Center's projects offer students an opportunity to identify the ways in which they can contribute. While architectural skills can play a role in advancing change, they cannot do it alone, and learning to identify other appropriate tools is an important skill.

The last two chapters in this book illustrate the Center's work as being future-oriented through small acts of relationship-building. "Cultivating Novel Partnerships and New Coalitions" describes how the Center connects multiple social and political networks in the city. Since it works at the intersection of institutional authority, operating within a university, and grassroots action, in dialogue with community-based groups, the Center is positioned to facilitate new collaborations. Informed by community activism, yet partnering with municipal and state entities, the Center has the opportunity to flip the script on how changes are traditionally advanced. Design is a tool the Center uses to envision an inclusive city and to catalyze that radical vision through a series of nimble actions.

Our last chapter, "Stewarding Small Steps toward Big Changes," demonstrates the importance of envisioning the city's future with wild imagination. Though the footprint of the Center's work is often small scale, the work contributes to organizations working toward big social transformations and radically different futures. Through process and product, the Center aims to prototype the social dynamics and physical design of a more just and sustainable future. In the face of climate change, our cities cannot continue the policies and approaches of the past. Architects bring tools that can help facilitate more imaginative ideas of urban life in the future.

Working in community means learning about the past from multiple–sometimes conflicting–histories. Working in community necessitates the significant labor of building new relationships and sustaining them over years. Working in community means taking seriously the creation of a city that is not just physically transformed but shaped by a recognition that there is strength in our interdependence. Learning to hold on to hope that the world can be more just, more equitable, and more beautiful is a radical proposition.

How do we step into uncertain and aspirational futures, while also attending to the real constraints and material needs of the day? Small Center's work demonstrates that hope and pragmatism can coexist when we work in partnership. The Center's design process shows the power of small actions that build and maintain a community: answering the call to help solve a problem, going to City Hall to help plead a case, showing up at a crawfish boil, or celebrating our neighbors' graduations and weddings. Small Center shapes the city through its dedication to the technical skill of high-quality design alongside the interpersonal skill of maintaining a consistent, caring presence. As Small Center's Emilie Taylor Welty often notes, for the Center's staff and collaborators, their work is more than just a design project: "This city is our home."

---

[1] Barbara Brown Wilson, *Resilience for All: Striving for Equity through Community-Driven Design* (Island Press, 2018), 20-23; Anna Goodman, "A History of Community Design/Build in the United States in Four Moments," in *Globalizing Architecture/Flows and Disruptions: Proceedings of the 102nd ACSA Annual Meeting*, ed. John Stuart and Mabel Wilson (ACSA Press, 2014).

[2] Zachary Lamb, "Connecting the Dots: The Origins, Evolutions, and Implications of the Map that Changed Post-Katrina Recovery Planning in New Orleans," in *Louisiana's Response to Extreme Weather: A Coastal State's Adaptation Challenges and Successes*, ed. Shirley Laska (Springer Open, 2020), 65-91.

[3] For more on URBANbuild, see Ila Berman and Mona El Khafif, *URBANbuild: local/global* (ORO Editions, 2009).

[4] Letter from the People of New Orleans to Our Friends and Allies, April 1, 2007, https://leftturn.org/letter-people-new-orleans-our-friends-and-allies/, also quoted in Suzanne-Juliette Mobley and Nick Jenisch, "Recovery to Resilience: Finding a Transdisciplinary Approach to Community-Based Design," *Conjunctions: Transdisciplinary Journal of Cultural Participation* 2, no. 2 (2015): 99-166, https://doi.org/10.7146/tjcp.v2i2.22922.

[5] Scott Bernhard, "Engagement, Ecology, and Design Education: Outreach Work of the Tulane City Center," *Innovations: Technology, Governance, Globalization* 5, no. 3 (2010): 91-105, https://doi.org/10.1162/INOV_a_00031.

Holy Ghost Houses: Freedom as Location, Scale, and Tempo

A Memoir Scaffolding Abolitionist Futurity in Two Acts[6]

Essay & Artwork by
Anna Livia Brand

Prologue: In The Wake
Location: 300 + 20 Flood Street

Flood Street is one of those New Orleans streets that runs perpendicular to the Mississippi River. It is an arpent, a remnant of the French cadastral plantation system of long, narrow lots fronting the river. As an urban infrastructure and propertied landscape, this plantation logic still underlies much of the city's footprint, including the Lower Ninth Ward, a landscape once plotted into sugar plantations over 300 years ago and one of the neighborhoods hit hardest by the levee failures of Hurricane Katrina twenty years ago. In the Lower Nine, Flood Street stretches from the Mississippi River all the way back to Florida Avenue and Bayou Bienvenue. At the River, it eases up to the top of the natural levee, providing access to the wharves along the river and the warehouses supporting these wharves. At Florida Avenue, Flood Street ends just before crossing the Norfolk Southern Railroad, which divides the Lower Ninth Ward from Bayou Bienvenue. As a transect across the Lower Ninth Ward, Flood Street works topographically, from high point to low point, and therefore historically, from dry ground to flooded ground.

Despite the (at times) topographical expressions of race across the city, Flood Street is a loose racial transect, a point that is generative for thinking about the indelibility of post-diluvial images, the nuances of racial geographies, and Black residents' insistence that freedom has a place in the post-Katrina landscape. In the Lower Ninth Ward, higher ground is whiter, lower ground is Blacker, but these distinctions are both relative, in a neighborhood that is predominantly Black, and

"In New Orleans, we tell direction by where we are in relation to the Mississippi River, in relation to water."
-Sarah M. Brown, The Yellow House

critical, in a neighborhood whose Black activism is rooted in the land and the sky of this beautiful place. It is Lower Nine residents who have always taught us what freedom must look like. It is Lower Nine residents who have always taught us how to claim and make home amidst any storm. Therefore, as much as Flood Street attests to the longue durée of Black and Indigenous oppression and emplaced/placeless vulnerability in and across the city, Flood Street is also a transect attesting to Lower Nine residents' wake work: wake work stretching back over 300 years; wake work renewed in the days, weeks and months following Katrina; wake work renewed twenty years ago and constantly taking part in the "unfinished project of emancipation." It is in this wake work where I locate the Albert and Tina Small Center's work. It is in this liminal space where the social, economic, and environmental dimensions of their community-based design can be understood as infrastructurally taking part in the geographical production of freedom. In the moment of the wake and in sites across the city, Small Center takes dreams and makes them a reality; makes tangible the hope of everyday folks.

In the wake of Hurricane Katrina, we have witnessed twenty years of incalculable efforts to make the city anew. This work has taken place through countless planning efforts and in countless meetings. Conversations have reached across tables in school gyms and auditoriums, have continued out onto the sidewalk and into community meetings. While much of rebuilding over the past twenty years has exposed the limits of urban planning and urban design to rebuild a racially and economically just city, the community scale visioning–the conversations that took place in folded chairs in an old Walgreens or an unflooded house and when residents were still trying to rebuild–those conversations are the kind that Small Center's work amplifies. Like the grander project of American democracy, New Orleans is a testament to the possibility of an idea that we can live together, that we can weather the storm, that we can come through to the other side. And it is in this infrastructure of hope and love that Small Center makes work.

The focus of this essay is on the ground of abolitionist thinking and the bones of futurity that still rest in the landscape. Drawing on temporal transects of Black abolitionist spatial praxes and inspired by Small Center's work across the city, I focus on how desire, joy, and love are expansive geographical formations that insist on a multitude of geographical possibilities of freedom. This essay is a generative memoir written in two acts, each of which imagines and conjures the contours, locations, and spaces of hope that Small Center takes part in. The first act works toward an argument against the diluvial dystopia that the post-Katrina city represents. Even now, twenty years after the storm, it is hard to loosen the hold that images of flooding, devastation, and abandonment have on a sense of hopeful futurity. And while we might annotate the pre- and post-Katrina landscape through a series of temporal, topographical, and socio-economic metrics produced by anti-Blackness, Black residents insist on other futures than ones these metrics foretell, insist on a world beyond (but including) mourning. We are, in contrast, taught by Black residents' insistence that locating hope requires the continued praxis of political and cultural placemaking; the inhabitance of sidewalks and stoops, streets and city hall; bars and porches; and the casting and scaling of desire to the post-Katrina story. This deeper, more hopeful yet still critical, deluge not only scales the unequal aftermaths of Katrina to a much deeper history, but also locates and scales the full depth and resonance of Black residents' dreams. The extraordinary things that residents have done in the wake of the storm, moments and places that Small Center has taken part in orchestrating, thus have historical resonance in the political praxis of making a home space. Residents' work and Small Center's part in making manifest these dreams, from the scale of a bench to the sale of a home to the scale of a village, contests images and metrics that propose only destruction. This is the scale, the place and the imagination from which abolition comes from.

The second act of this memoir begins with the conclusion of the first, though it solidifies residents' contestation of racial geographical formations by calling on the generations of activism and Black placemaking that preceded Katrina. However, goal of the second memoir is not refutation. It is toward hope, toward freedom, toward joy. Therefore, it takes the *longue durée* of residents' activism as the ground of abolition and, thinking with residents' work, suggests the inescapability of freedom. It focuses on the infrastructural and material dimensions of hope, locating Small Center's work as a material and symbolic distinction in the landscape still becoming the possible ground of freedom. A final Epilogue offers love toward the city for the next 300 years.

Act One: The First Line and Cutting the Body Loose, 2005
The Dirge House, 1865 Lamentation and Hope, High Ground of the Mississippi

The Grand Marshall steps to the left, his right foot joining before swaying to the right. Slowly marking time and space. The dirge is a form of honoring the dead. It is the moment of mourning before letting go. In this ghost house, we mourn the loss of those we have loved. We lament the moments we must pick up and move on away from those we lost. We touch the ground with our feet, hold soil in our hands, let water flow through our fingers. We see the reflections of those we love in the arc of a tuba in the band passing by. We see the shadows shift on the ground beneath our feet, some of them from ghosts of trees and some from newly planted ones. We remember that this mourning is critical to hope; that in New Orleans, this has always been done, and that to change the tempo, we have to understand and mark who and what has passed on.

The jazz funeral passes the Dirge House, a slow movement along Lamentation Street and toward Hope. The slow pace marks each instance that we were lost to one another, that families have been taken from one another. It marks those who could not return home after Katrina, who

A country neighborhood. A levee. Dawn.[9]

never returned home hundreds of years before. Residents stand on the weathered steps leading up to the porch of the still standing, still mighty Dirge House. Residents stand on the concrete steps next door, where no one has returned. The crowd of mourners pass the line of empty steps, pass the homes coming back, their loved ones rebuilding board by board, memory by memory. Residents bow their heads to let this moment pass and in doing so, they remember the water, the laughter, the hearts singing. They recall the sound of someone coming home, someone calling out to them saying, I love you, saying, come back now. They gather to mourn, to mark the time and hold the moment. This marking the time and the absence of someone lost, of something lost, of something ending, is not new in New Orleans. This praxis stretches back, at least until 1865 when, at the Holy Name of Jesus Church on North Claiborne Avenue and Ursulines Street, Black residents from across the city took part in a two-day jazz funeral for slavery. Residents then celebrated the "Death of American Slavery" (*Mort de l'esclavage Americain*). Residents then gathered in a mass of solemn jubilation (*messe solonnelle de Jubilation*), burying and throwing dirt upon the monster, "the infamy" (*l'infame*) of slavery. Residents now mourn other lives and loves lost to some new aqueous monster.

Marking the end of slavery was one moment in the long walk toward emancipation. There have been countless moments, countless jazz funerals since. Each one gathers traditions into the streets and in the fall of footsteps on the sacred ground, the everyday ground. This is remembrance. Each one weaves together a line through neighborhoods, connecting the ephemerality of life with death, of place to place. Each one claims space, claims life lines and pathways for living cultural praxes, and claims the moment and possibility of rupture, the break between this and that. And while we know that the death-dealing dimensions of racial geographies have continued to form in the wake of 1865, just as they have in the wake of Katrina, the Dirge House is a site where mourning and lamentation are mixed with hope and with the labor of vision. Residents will sit on this porch. They will talk and conjure memories of life before and of those no longer here. They will share drinks and cry while laughing and laugh while crying. They will go back inside and get to work. Thus, the Dirge House, by still standing, is not only a house of mourning. It is where hope is formed out of the bones of what has passed and what can be remembered. Here you find residents, in the wake of mourning and in the formative shoals hope, doing the careful work of re-membering toward a different future.

In the empty lots, in the front steps without a home, and in the absence of those still not returned is a reminder of work still being done. The deluge of Katrina left behind destruction. This was and is clear. It marked a moment when race was made anew and this is something of no small consequence. What is also clear is that rebuilding, marking the moment between what was and what might become, was one steeped in a more deeply faceted tone and tempo of anti-Blackness, a historical arc that links back to and from the origins of enslavement and its ensuing spatial logics. New Orleans' racial geography is not unlike the segregated fabrics of the American South and much of the United States. And while the deluge marked new forms of dispossession and exclusion, New Orleans is perhaps like nowhere else and this, I want to suggest, is one of the primary ways that Small Center's work is uniquely situated in a material and symbolic sense. Rather than take the post-diluvial geography for granted, the Center's work has woven itself into the fabric of lamenting the as is of racial geographical formations while dreaming the world anew. It "cut[s] the groove the other way" where "a variety of possibilities emerge beyond just thinking about chocolate cities as silos of socially and spatially isolated Blackness." It takes part in imagining new "lifeworlds social, economic, and political places of dynamism and great consequence." The Dirge House is the where this consequential hope is forged.

Thus, this conjured space of the Dirge House is one figurative space where Small Center's work gains resonance. Just as the dirge locates lamentation and hope in the same moment, the Center's advocacy, visioning, coalition and home building (all of which are woven across sites, across the city), locate and shift the geographical consequences of hope wherever they gain figurative and material ground. While the Center's work could be counted in numbers, I want to suggest that each site, each community-grounded effort, is enfolded in these deeper praxes of liberation that have taken place before and since Katrina. In this sense, the Center's work becomes scaled in the spatiality of freedom building, a process that arcs backward and forward and across the city. Small Center takes part in shaping the infrastructural materiality of hope, while not losing site of the necessary work of this hope being drawn from and out of these moments and spaces of lamentation and joy. Thus, the materiality of claiming space through outdoor classrooms, new homes, and gathering spaces; through mobile markets that bring new food traditions to the stoops of communities; and through installations that remember and reconnect history are the ways through which Small Center makes manifest the dreams of residents. Small Center cannot and does not do their work without residents, and this is perhaps one of the most important dimensions of their contributions to the wake of Katrina. By insisting that beauty lies in residents' everyday imaginary, Small Center climbs the steps, walks into the Dirge House, and takes part in the moment between lamentation and hope. They take part in building new futures, in grounding liberation. This is their wake work.

Act Two: The Second Lines of Freedom, 2025
The Desire House, 2005 Hope and Liberation

Once the moment passes, once the body is buried, once the coffin is settled into the ground, the tempo shifts. Now it is an upbeat tempo that celebrates life and insists we are not only haunted, not only disciplined by the nightmares of loss but also alive, also in love, also in conversation with each other and with many possible futures. If Small Center's work is

...what is not lost is paradise[15]

wake work, it is also work where new textures of hope gain infrastructural traction. It is also where and when the importance of liberation takes generative form. They take part in weaving new configurations of hope.

In many ways, Small Center's work can be understood in the materialities of these configurations and what they then make possible. When you live in New Orleans, you live within the traces of history at the same time that you live with the constant textures of life. A concrete stoop is sloped and marked by the hundreds of feet that have passed this threshold. A wood porch is worn down by folks sitting and talking, sharing the everyday, forging new possibilities in the space between their words, their sorrows, and their joy. The side of a house is marked in all of the colors someone once celebrated. The bricks were formed by hands hundreds of years ago. The wood floors that were first laid down even before emancipation are now where your children run, their laughter echoing off the yellow plaster walls, the sunlight streaming through the transom. Your front stoop is where you connect with others. Your back stoop might be the stepping off place to a new gathering. The ground glimmers with broken mirrors and oyster shells. The shade is necessary, the levee beautiful.

At every turn in New Orleans's generous neighborhoods, the second line can make space. It can conjure a dimension of joy that is expansive, that is undiminishable. When the second line passes the Desire House, everyone comes outside, everyone joins in because this is what New Orleans teaches you: joy is something that must be practiced together, is something of substance and the press of your foot on the ground. From the Desire House, old and new souls pour out from their work and their praxes to make anew the sounds of the street and the claims that life can have on space. The second line might take us away, might transport us down the street, might show us different ways a woman can express beauty in her footwork. A second line takes you from home, only to return you home as someone different. We don't return to the Desire House as we were before, we return in the arms of joy to a space we now see as one colored by hope and liberation. The pale-yellow walls are now textured by sunlight. The shadows of trees now moving musically. The wood floors now seem more solid beneath our feet, feet that just touched the solid ground, feet that just walked back home.

This is also where we can understand the work of Small Center, in the ways that it makes possible spaces of gathering and coming together. It is this coming together, whether on a stoop or in a public space, where the shift from hope toward liberation gains ground. My sense of the Center's work, much like my sense of life while living in New Orleans, is that in the spaces it helps materialize, gathering freedom is made possible. While this praxis, much like that of jazz funerals, has a deep history across Black cultural spaces, the making anew in the footwork of a dream or the welding of a shade structure or the joining of wood for a new bookcase is a substantive shift in the work of freedom. Footwork marks the beat in creative and joyful ways. Shade brings people together in respite and therefore in generative rest and refuge. Bookshelves house the books that teach children to dream. As spaces of substantive dreaming, everyday life on the streets, sidewalks, and spaces of New Orleans's Black neighborhoods teaches us is that freedom is an admix, a constant configuration and constellation of hope. For Small Center, this admix is rooted in the process of engaged design. This is literal and symbolic work and the spaces that Small Center helps facilitate cannot be conditioned by predetermined outcomes. These spaces create cascades of possibilities, where residents and communities keep making and keep weaving. Much like Black New Orleans's political and cultural praxes are rooted in a deeply generative creativity, Small Center partners to create spaces that are themselves generative of new configurations, new beats, new tempos, and new moments.

The Desire House is one way of thinking about Small Center's work. This is space is made of wood and nails, of bricks and plaster, or color and sunlight. This space is made through conversation and memory work, in the refusal to forget and in the hopeful stance of marking one's return home. The center takes part in residents' work to make manifest a new home, the promise that many residents spray painted on their walls in the wake of the storm. "This was home. This is home." This will be home. Desire is what takes up the hammer and nails. Desire chooses a color. Desire determines the scale and materiality of gathering spaces.

"We all live somewhere." -Mark Bradford[19]

Desire is both the intention and the destination. We have hope in this labor. We have hope in the work that the Center takes part in.

Epilogue: Holy Ghost Houses
Location: 20 + 300

New Orleans residents locate desire in tangible, everyday ways. They make possible hope even in the wake of the deluge, even in the relentless pounding of racialized storms. This hope is substantive. It is not just something we cling to naively, it is something we cling to with a generative belief in love and our collective capacity to make love manifest, to let love shift these confines of dispossession and oppression. Living there, both before and after the storm, is at once the most powerful and critical celebration of the capacity of love, from the smallest expressions of stoop conversations to the more expansive expressions of insisting on racial equality and freedom for every doorstep, every porch, and every resident. Living there is learning about liberation and its unfinished work.

The gift of Small Center is that it takes part in locating the possible geographies of freedom, placing them in conversation with new futures. Its work is a love song to the city—to its residents and to their futures. In its own way, the Center makes possible the next 300 years, whatever diluvial challenges those years might bring. While tracking what needs mending, what needs attention, it also builds, it also creates. It dreams with residents and therefore, makes love as geographical possibility.

---

[6] The title for this essay takes its inspiration from a number of sources. First, it draws inspiration from Small Center's residential project, Holy Ghost House, located in Central City. This essay also reads Cheryl Harris's *Whiteness as Property* and *In the Shadow of Plessy* as foundational texts for thinking about the Lower Ninth Ward twenty years after Katrina. Further, it draws inspiration from two works by artist Mark Bradford. The first is his installation, *Mithra* (2008), which was sited in the Lower Ninth Ward as part of Prospect 3 New Orleans Biennial. The second work is his large-scale painting, *Corner of Desire and Piety* (2008), which focuses on deliveries of propane to FEMA trailers in New Orleans. Next, it draws inspiration from Chandra McCormick and Keith Calhoun's *Memoirs of the Lower*

Ninth Ward (2023), an installation in the Lower Ninth Ward for Prospect 6 New Orleans Biennial. Finally, and because I have been working in the format of a play in a different project, it draws on artist Paul Chan's staging of Samuel Beckett's *Waiting for Godot* in 2007 in post-Katrina New Orleans, part of which was staged in the Lower Ninth Ward. While I draw on these inspirations throughout the text, the research is grounded in my own years of research and work in New Orleans and the Lower Ninth Ward. Ultimately, this essay, which draws on my own learning from New Orleans's residents, is one where I am learning with Small Center's efforts to make anew the possibilities of freedom.

[7] I'm drawing on Ruth Wilson Gilmore's assertion that "freedom is a place." See Ruth Wilson Gilmore, *Abolition Geography: Essays Towards Liberation* (Verso, 2022).

[8] Christina Sharpe, *In the Wake: On Blackness and Being* (Duke University Press, 2016), 5.

[9] Samuel Beckett, *Waiting for Godot* (Les Éditions de Minuit, 1952).

[10] Greg A. Beamen, "The Claiborne Avenue History Project Wants New Orleanians to Share their Memories of Historic Street," *The New Orleans Tribune*, April 30, 2019, https://theneworleanstribune.com/2019/04/30/the-claiborne-avenue-history-project-wants-new-orleanians-to-share-their-memories-of-historic-street/?fbclid=IwY2xjawFIKgZleHRuA2FlbQIxMAABHRllEYGlL7Ko1YVMPDcfp-0hxvJU7sbzyn7QbgQvqRc8tijG5GfP0-mY2Q_aem_T7D3O3sf5RlrGSyLQ2gI6Q.

[11] Rinaldo Walcott, *The Long Emancipation: Walking Toward Black Freedom* (Duke University Press, 2021).

[12] Lauret Savoy, *Trace: Memory, History, Race, and the American Landscape* (Counterpoint Press, 2016); Tiffany Lethabo King, *The Black Shoals: Offshore Formations of Black and Native Studies* (Duke University Press, 2019).

[13] Marcus Anthony Hunter and Zandria F. Robinson, *Chocolate Cities: The Black Map of American Life* (University of California Press, 2018).

[14] Hunter and Robinson, *Chocolate Cities*, 178.

[15] Excerpted from Lucille Clifton, "Monday Sundown 9/17/01, Rosh Hashanah," *September Suite* (American Academy of Poets, 2001).

[16] Toni Morrison, "Rootedness: The Ancestor as Foundation," *Black Women Writers (1950-1980): A Critical Evaluation*, ed. Mari Evans (Anchor Press/Doubleday, 1984).

[17] Isabelle Anguelovski, *Neighborhood as Refuge Community Reconstruction, Place Remaking, and Environmental Justice in the City* (The MIT Press, 2014).

[18] Marked on a home in the Lower Ninth Ward, 2005.

[19] Mark Bradford, "Mark Bradford on Prospect.1 New Orleans," *Art21 Magazine*, December 12, 2014, https://magazine.art21.org/2014/12/12/mark-bradford-on-prospect-1-new-orleans/.

SECTION ONE

Learning From a Social City

1

Gathering with Communities

"With different modes of exploration and exchange in proximity, new possibilities for interdisciplinary learning and collaboration are discovered."

New Orleans culture is known for food, spectacle, and celebration. In keeping with the city's spirit of camaraderie, Small Center hosts events that invite diverse groups to engage in conversations about the city. Small Center sees this tradition as an integral part of the collaborative design process, recognizing that holding space for joy and fellowship builds support for design change. The Center's "community storefront" space hosts public programming focused on issues of the built environment. The space brings together artists, makers, students, and non-profit organizations into dialogue, while ensuring local neighborhood leaders direct these conversations.

In 2014, Small Center moved to an off-campus building that facilitates studios, classes, and design-build projects. However, the space represents much more. Located in New Orleans' Central City neighborhood, it is close to many of the Center's nonprofit partners, accessible by car or public transit, and serves as a central place for gathering, discussion, and collaboration. The community storefront space gives Small Center an outward-facing presence. It houses exhibits in partnership with nonprofits and artists, but also allows partners to hold their own events, from documentary screenings to organizational retreats. The space helps Small Center maintain a visual presence and serves as a place to expand connections and envision a better future.

For ten years, Small Center has hosted exhibits and events tied to its design projects and the work of its partners. The storefront space serves as an embodiment of the

Center and a symbol of its stability, accessibility, and commitment to community-based work. Food, drinks, and interactive programming draw a wide variety of participants. Small Center's many partner organizations bring their extended networks to the space. The result is a dynamic–if sometimes chaotic–working environment that can accommodate everything from a beading workshop by a local Mardi Gras Indian chief to a panel discussion on the history of Black labor and its impact on the built environment.

Exhibits are typically interdisciplinary, connecting the work of grassroots organizations, artists, and youth participants. The space has also been used by partner organizations for their own programming, meetings, and retreats. The full potential of the Center is realized through these overlapping uses. On a given day, a design studio might be making prototypes in the wood shop and testing them in the storefront space while a team of students and faculty is working with a partner on graphics about safe housing conditions and the Center staff are standing up an exhibit about affordable housing. With the different modes of exploration and exchange in proximity, new possibilities for interdisciplinary learning and collaboration are organically discovered.

The Center has completed over 160 projects in its twenty-year history, alongside innumerable informal efforts: providing design expertise, realizing built projects, facilitating engagement and strategizing, creating graphic advocacy, and more. Beyond individual design projects, the engagement process itself can provide lasting and meaningful change. In 2020, Small Center worked with an outside researcher to anonymously interview past project partners to quantify the impact of engaged design projects and processes. The effort captured sentiments from partners that highlighted the value of the engagement process, with impacts reaching beyond design results. As one interviewee put it:

> Our clients would question why they were going to work with designers: [there was an] assumption that 'there won't be care[,'] and [they were] telling us[,] 'We have actively NOT sought out designers, architects, historic preservation because of the racist history of design'. But by the end (of working with Center), we changed that! So many clients were saying[,] 'I too am now a historic preservationist'. That's huge![20]

The engagement process aims to build long-term relationships with nonprofit and community partners while educating the next generation of socially conscious and technically competent designers. The process is based on simple actions: listening closely, asking questions to get the full story, and developing ideas in dialogue. Students learn firsthand the value of bringing people together to tackle real issues. Each project is an opportunity for stakeholders to engage in shaping the future of the city.

These exchanges occur in structured design reviews and focus groups but also include the informal conversations after public events or during site visits. Gathering people together is a core tool for engagement at Small Center, whether it is planned around

a design project, a pressing policy issue, or in celebration of neighborhood histories and cultural traditions. Small Center's work is grounded in the idea that responding to current needs and valuing small-scale wins aggregates into a big impact over time. Even while responding in the moment, the Center strives to keep an eye on long-term trends of equity, access, and social justice. The overall effect of this incremental progress is possible because of the Center's organizational partners: groups that are often small in number, but whose work is nevertheless big in impact. Past and present partners have housed those without shelter, grown fresh, local food for communities without access to it, provided youth activities and job training, and much more. Small Center brings value by enhancing the dedicated efforts of its partners, and it is this potential to increase their impact that gives meaning to the Center's work.

The key to building relationships and networks is to convene community members consistently and strategically throughout the design process. Different participants need different outlets to make their voices heard; the most comfortable platform for a nonprofit partner may not be the same as for a member of the public. Recognizing this, the Center hosts multiple events to reach multiple constituencies. Regular meetings are also critical in refining designs to best serve the needs of the partner organization. There must be a continuous feedback loop during the design process, and even an opportunity to adjust on-site as built projects take shape. The act of gathering again and again, in small and large groups, in different formats and settings, ensures the efficacy of the final design. It also facilitates parallel conversations about safety and sustainability, and technical concerns like utilities and maintenance. Multiple conversations and formats ensure all issues are well-considered and frankly discussed.

Small Center has served as a conduit for community-based project ideas from its beginning, when it connected thinkers with resources in the wake of Hurricane Katrina. The goal then was to provide design and engagement expertise for projects identified by nonprofits and community groups, rather than researching purely academic interests or building speculative projects without specific users in mind. This practical approach allowed Small Center to define its projects in response to community concerns as they arose on a year-to-year basis, the changes in the Center's workflow sometimes providing insight into changes in local needs or approaches. One year, multiple urban agriculture projects were proposed, while affordable housing efforts emerged in the next.

Small Center formalized this process into an annual Request for Proposals (RFP) in 2010. The RFP aimed to accomplish several goals: democratizing and organizing requests for pro-bono design services; involving community leaders and nonprofit partners in project selection as jury members; and solidifying the Center's ability to gauge needs and trends across the city. The Center designed the RFP process with equal access in mind. The application is intentionally brief and designed to encourage entries. Not only is the RFP outreach conducted online, but to reach community members who lack internet access the RFP is distributed through posters, fliers, and word of mouth. The Center staff holds information sessions for those interested, outlining the process and reviewing draft proposals before the submission date.

The RFP process is still a credit to the Small Center's engagement process today. Gathering proposals centrally and at a single time gives Small Center the ability to plan for a coming year of projects while accommodating academic schedules. Yearly proposals also allow the Center to adapt to changing needs in the city by assembling different permutations of faculty and experts suited to the needs at hand. Each year's jury includes a combination of community members, past project partners, students, and faculty members who review and rank proposals, typically twenty to thirty per cycle. Small Center has developed an assessment matrix that quantifies: (1) a project's need, identified by its potential impact on challenging inequitable systems and increasing equity; (2) a project's educational value, or whether the project provides ample design and education opportunities for students; and (3) a project's sustainability, as defined by Small Center's ability to execute a project and the partner's ability to maintain a built project or advance a visioning project. The RFP process is the first step in building trust with potential partners and the communities they serve.

In keeping with New Orleans's identity as a social city, Small Center has taken the time to build networks the old-fashioned way: sharing food and space, participating in mutual aid, organizing and serving as a connector, and, of course, by providing design services where needed. Community is built through ritual and friendship. These were always part of the Center's DNA but have expanded through twenty years of partnerships and the move to a neighborhood-based space. The projects and guest essays that follow illustrate how special events and open gatherings have provided opportunities for convening community conversations, with impacts that continue well beyond a project's construction.

"We're people people."[21] -Ronald Lewis, The House of Dance and Feathers

[20] Anonymous Interview with past Small Center project partner, 2019-2021.

[21] Dan Baum, "Death and Life in New Orleans," *The American Prospect*, February 20, 2009, https://prospect.org/online-extras/death-life-new-orleans/.

EVENT

Reinhabiting NOLA

Connecting to Local Needs, 2005

Though Small Center formed before levee failures destroyed much of New Orleans, the Center found early purpose in helping to organize the global response to Hurricane Katrina. The Center facilitated exchanges between communities identifying their own problems and those with the professional expertise to tackle them. This focus on connection has carried through the Center's work to the present day. The Center uses gatherings and face-to-face conversations to bring resources to immediate needs and to work toward long-term, systemic change.

During the city's recovery efforts, members of the architecture and design community, including practitioners and leaders at schools of architecture, wondered how they could help. Many flocked to the city in the early months, gutting and repairing houses with an eye on longer-term design needs. Small Center acted as a matchmaker by pairing offers of help with local groups facing architectural needs.

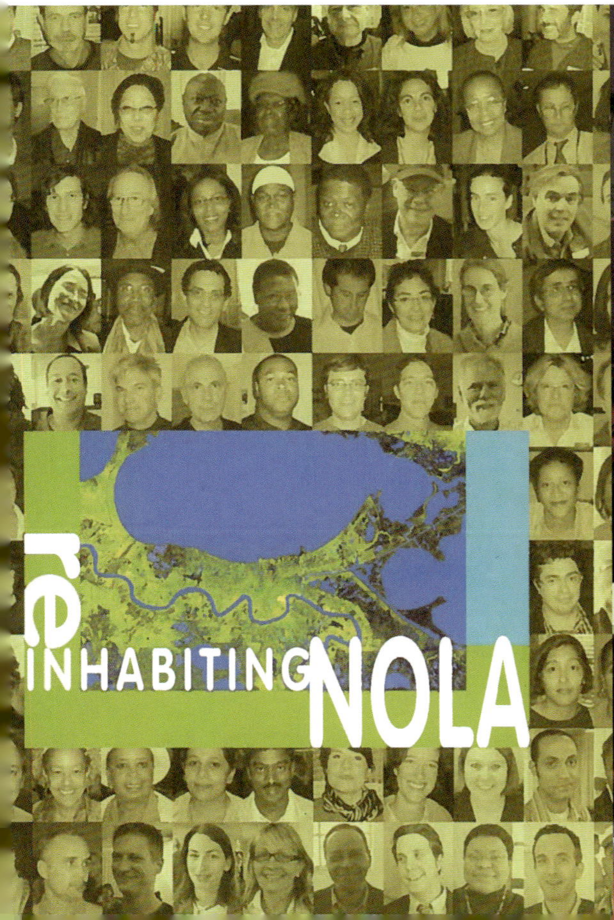

The Center also participated in citywide recovery planning efforts and co-convened architecture-specific gatherings. In November 2005, Tulane School of Architecture and Built Environment, Xavier University, and the Tulane/Xavier Center for Bioenvironmental Research hosted the Reinhabiting NOLA Conference. With national media attention on the disaster beginning to wane, the conference aimed to establish a framework for ongoing community participation in recovery planning for the city. The goal of the conference was to pool a diversity of expertise and experience to enact a culturally appropriate vision for the long-term recovery of New Orleans neighborhoods. The event linked community and government representatives with architectural resources. It established priorities grounded in social and environmental justice, with high quality design at the core. These priorities shaped Small Center's work in the months that followed.

The University of Arkansas hosted a follow-up conference in December 2005, which resulted in the formation of the CITYbuild Consortium of Schools.[22] Participating design and planning schools sought the most effective response to the overwhelming cleanup and rebuilding needs. The idea for the CITYbuild program emerged as the group recognized that to effectively help with such an enormous disaster, they would need to work together over time. As the New Orleans coordinator of CITYbuild, Small Center organized multi-disciplinary collaborations and coordinated work in

concentrated areas.[23] CITYbuild's goal was to exponentially increase every individual effort to meet the scale of the need. By the end of 2006, CITYbuild participants included thirty national and international design programs, representing sixty faculty, more than 600 students, and twenty local, community organizations. The results of these partnerships included approximately sixteen built or rehabilitated structures and more than 200 design and architecture proposals.

Eventually, CITYbuild was put into a "dormant phase" to be re-established in the aftermath of future crises. The consortium prototyped a model for inter-university collaboration applicable to other urban contexts whenever disaster might strike.

CITYbuild was only one outgrowth of the Reinhabiting NOLA conference; one of Small Center's first major projects also emerged from conversations at that gathering. This project addressed the issue of "adjudicated properties." Land parcels with delinquent taxes that have not sold at tax sales are "adjudicated," or given to the city. Vacant land, whether predating Hurricane Katrina or created by it, posed both recovery challenges and opportunities. To actively use these empty parcels, the city needed to understand what it owned. However, in these early months of recovery, this was unclear. By talking with university partners and organizations on the ground, the Center was able to construct a map of adjudicated properties in selected zones across New Orleans.

Supported by the Fannie Mae Foundation, Small Center hosted a summit in February 2006 focused on the issue. In attendance were City of New Orleans agency leadership, local professionals, and experts from the National Vacant Properties Campaign. Attendees established a method for the City of New Orleans to document such parcels. The process synthesized information from several city agencies, supplementing existing data with field documentation of property conditions and current photographs. The effort provided one of the first clear pictures of the redevelopment challenges to come. The work begun at the summit eventually led to initiatives to mitigate municipal blight and vacancy like Lot Next Door and Mow to Own.

[22] Patrick Rhodes, "Casting our Buckets Down," in *Re.Building: Proceedings of the 98th ACSA Annual Meeting*, ed. Bruce Goodwin and Judith Kinnard (ACSA Press, 2010), 151-156.
[23] Doug Harmon, "Groundworks 2006 review, CITYbuild consortium of schools – URBANbuild prototype," *ACSA News 36*, no. 4 (2006): 18.

VISIONING

Ride New Orleans

Visualizing Improvements to Public Transportation, 2014

Gathering can be an act of community, learning, caring, and celebration. However, gathering can also look like activism or direct action. As a part of the University, the Center does not take direct policy positions, but the Center's research on complex issues helps inform conversations and highlight challenges. Small Center has worked with several nonprofit partners advocating for changes to municipal policies on housing, transit, and land use. The Center graphically describes policies that shape the built environment and visually demonstrates ideas for change.

In one such project, Small Center worked with Ride New Orleans, a transit advocacy organization, to create a report entitled, "Smart Transit for a Strong Economy: Why New Orleans Should Invest in a CBD Transit Hub. " The project studied transit mobility issues and highlighted the opportunity to improve access by creating transit-centric

// ABOVE: City leaders gather in support of improved transportation
// OPPOSITE: The project studied all public transit routes to find critical nodes and efficiencies

public spaces at critical intersections. Small Center created maps and visualized the design of public amenities to illustrate gaps in the City's transit routes and possible solutions. The study focused on an area in New Orleans's Central Business District where more than twenty regional transit lines converged, functioning as a transit hub for 5,000 riders each day. Ride New Orleans conducted surveys of riders about their transit experiences. The report summarized the concerns raised by riders using comments, photographs, and maps. The graphics clarified how transit lines connected, illustrating the confusing number of transfers and stops in the area. The report concluded that the area lacked the basic amenities to make it a safe and pleasant public space for commuters.

Small Center collected historic precedents and case studies from around the U.S. as possible models for a new transit hub in the CBD. To make civic investment in public space financially viable, featured solutions leveraged funding opportunities and partnerships. The report also presented the idea of a transit hub in the CBD as an opportunity to express civic pride while creating new, smart development opportunities in a strategic location. Additionally, the report presented key intersections where transfers currently happen and visualized changes to these dangerous intersections to create safer spaces for bus and streetcar passengers. The design proposals identified alternative intersections across the public transit system in New Orleans.

On the day of the report's release, Ride New Orleans organized a Day of Action. They set up 200 folding chairs at South Rampart Street, the proposed site of the CBD transit hub, responding to survey respondents who highlighted the lack of seating at bus stops. The temporary installation provided a place for riders to sit and demonstrated that there was ample space for seating. City Council members Susan Guidry, Kristin Palmer, LaToya Cantrell and James Grey attended to commit their support, alongside allied organizations, Stand with Dignity and the Amalgamated Transit Union Women of Action. Local media amplified the message.

The campaign directly led to new municipal investments. Shortly after the Day of Action, the Regional Transit Authority Board of Commissioners supported a planning study for locating a permanent, centralized downtown transit center. Since then, benches have been installed along Elk Place and South Rampart Street, giving waiting transit riders much-needed seating, and the sidewalk in front of a busy bus stop on South Rampart Street has been expanded.

EVENT

Red Beans Roundtables

Conversations about the Big Issues of a Small City, 2014 - 2019

Gathering as activism or protest is often imagined in public spaces, marches, or on the steps of City Hall. But early organizing often happens on front stoops, in kitchens, and in backyards across the city.

When Small Center expanded into its Baronne Street building in 2014, a new "community storefront" represented an opportunity to host events, educational teach-ins, and other public programming. The Center's move from approximately 200 square feet of office space into a 7500-square-foot building meant that each new room, the community storefront, classroom, studio space, and woodshop, offered new opportunities for collaboration. Located in Central City, a space physically closer to many nonprofit partners, the new building solved the difficulties of parking and building access often present on campus.

// ABOVE: Panelists discuss the housing crisis in New Orleans
// OPPOSITE: City leaders, developers, and designers play a zoning and housing game

While the move to a dedicated building came with significant and long-term funding implications, its effect on Small Center's ability to engage cannot be overstated. Before this move, Small Center had to rely on institutional partners' spaces to host events and exhibits. The Baronne Street building represented a new opportunity to produce exhibits, develop public programs, build relationships, and offer gathering space to nonprofit partners and community groups.

If you know New Orleans, you know the tradition of making and sharing a pot of red beans on Mondays. After moving into its new Baronne Street location, Small Center translated this tradition into a monthly discussion forum in its storefront space. A long-running series of panel discussions and forums explored local issues of architecture, policy, and planning. Red Beans Roundtables convened and, importantly, expanded Small Center's network of urbanists, nonprofit leaders, policymakers, and engaged residents. It also served to display and convey academic research in an accessible, public-facing way, so that it could contribute to ongoing discussions of pressing issues.

Small Center provided food and invited panelists with unique insights into each month's theme. The series brought together scholars and practitioners and built a strong core audience of civic leaders while remaining accessible to students and the general public. Based on the Center's belief that everyone brings expertise to the table, the Roundtables were an effort to learn, teach, and eat together. Panelists gave their answers to questions shared in advance, in a conversational format. However, they were also asked to bring their own questions, often finding answers from audience members. Discussions regularly went well past advertised event times. New partnerships formed and attendees resolved to move the work forward in subsequent meetups.

Some Red Beans Roundtables ran independently, but many were developed in conjunction with curated exhibits in the storefront space. For example, a series of Roundtables during *The Cost of Home* exhibit, discussed in Chapter 2, explored the local housing affordability crisis. Conversations centered on topics such as the city's work on fair housing policy, research on community investment trusts, and the local impacts of the Department of Housing and Urban Development. Another exhibit, *Sites of Resistance*, told the history of protest in New Orleans, and invited attendees to contribute by marking contemporary examples on an interactive map of the city. The opening event included a lively, facilitated discussion of past and current resistance movements in the city.

Supported for five years by the Surdna Foundation, Red Beans Roundtables and the storefront exhibits informed concurrent Small Center research and design projects.

Alongside *The Cost of Home* exhibit, the Center worked with the nonprofits, Greater New Orleans Housing Alliance (GNOHA) and the Greater New Orleans Fair Housing Action Center (GNOFHAC, now the Louisiana Fair Housing Action Center). Small Center helpled create graphics for GNOHA's inaugural report card on how the city was responding to a severe shortage of affordable housing. The Center's partnership with GNOFHAC developed their campaign for a rental registry, an attempt to create safe and healthy rental housing across the city (described in Chapter 4). Research and design for both efforts contributed to *The Cost of Home* exhibit, while the exhibit provided opportunities for both project partners to speak publicly about the issues they were tackling.

Red Beans Roundtables succeeded in gathering a recurring audience of municipal, nonprofit, community, and academic leaders each month. The events established the identity of the Baronne Street location as a consistent presence through regular programming, building on Small Center's reputation as a reliable public resource. However, because each exhibit required original research, curation, and the development of images and text, more recent programming has integrated guest artists and nonprofit partners as co-curators. This model is described in the section that follows.

Water Isn't a Game

Exploring the City's Relationship with Water, 2020

In Spring 2020, Small Center launched a new public programming series entitled DEPART-MENT, a nod to the history of the Center's Baronne Street building as part of the Kaufman's Department Store. *Water Isn't a Game* represented the first instantiation of the Center's new model for public exhibits, wherein nonprofit partners shaped exhibits as co-curators. Each exhibit featured the work of local artists alongside academic research. Artists were either invited to participate based on their body of work or applied for partnership through a juried selection process. The effort envisioned Small Center as a launch pad for collective learning, hoping to propel New Orleans towards a more enriching, equitable, and connected world. Blurring the lines between academia, community, and art allowed Small Center to expand its programming to reach audiences previously out of its orbit. Like Red Beans Roundtables, the new format aimed to create a nexus for new ideas, coalitions,

// ABOVE & OPPOSITE: Collaborators and exhibit visitors discuss and explore the challenges of water management in New Orleans

and civic action on issues related to the built environment, all in service to a city where every resident feels empowered to shape the places they live, work, and play.

Water Isn't a Game brought together research into, art about, and organizations centered on hydrology. The exhibit provided a picture of the flooding, subsidence, climactic, and other water-related threats to the city. In partnership with a local nonprofit, The Water Collaborative, and its director, Jessica Dandridge, the exhibit featured an interactive video installation designed to explore how people learn about, and engage with, stormwater management, using games, technology, design thinking, and art. "Living with Hurricanes," a Tulane School of Architecture seminar led by Aron Chang, developed research and prototypes for interactive educational displays for the exhibit. Work of students in Small Center's Public Interest Design seminar complemented *Waterlogged,* a photography and mixed media exhibit curated by local photographer and Small Center Collaborative Design Project Manager Jose Cotto. By incorporating multiple perspectives, the exhibit cultivated a diverse and holistic perspective on the built environment, aiming to inform future responses to changing water levels.

Water Isn't a Game brought together community partners, designers, environmental specialists and students to reshape the way New Orleanians think about water.

The opening event succeeded in attracting a diverse cross section of New Orleans residents and set a new high for event attendance. Attendees were eager to engage with the exhibit—all activities were hands-on, experiential, and could be enjoyed by multiple age groups. The exhibit provided opportunities for intergenerational learning and allowed visitors to explore their own relationship with water, some recalling personal experiences with storms and life in a floodplain.

Shortly after the opening of *Water Isn't a Game*, the Covid-19 pandemic led to the shutdown of public events, and Small Center's programming shifted to online forums. Audiences quickly tired of virtual meetings and Small Center staff developed creative ways to host events, including outdoor engagement and programming. This spirit of creativity still animates the Center's recent programming, which is co-created with local artists and aims to amplify the voice, concerns, and expertise of community partners.

Forging Paths from Crisis to Community

Dan Etheridge

The former Small Center co-director shares the ways in which early collaborations and deep partner knowledge helped to shape the Center's work over time.

The concept for Small Center had been kicked around for a little while during the early parts of 2005. Still new as Dean, Reed Kroloff brought the basic concept with him when he took the job at Tulane School of Architecture. His reasons were varied for creating place-based research center but focused on the fact that students who studied architecture at Tulane needed many more opportunities to learn from and contribute to the rich and exceptional built environment of New Orleans.

In his closing remarks at the Reinhabiting NOLA symposium hosted by Tulane School of Architecture (TSA) and the Tulane/Xavier Center for Bioenvironmental Research (CBR), Reed announced that he would be launching the Center on the back of the previous two days' proceedings. It is essential to look at the purpose, intent,

methods, and outcomes from that symposium to understand the Center's founding values.

In the months before Hurricane Katrina, I enjoyed working across a novel set of collaborations between environmental scientists at the CBR, architects and urban designers at TSA, and communication professionals at ePrime (an initiative co-founded by local publisher Kevin McCaffrey and Architect Alan Eskew). Our principal focus was to better understand how to improve built environment conditions in New Orleans against the backdrop of an eroding coastal wetland plain and a predicted increase in the intensity and frequency of strong hurricanes.

We had conceptualized an event that would speculate on the future of New Orleans in fifty years. The premise was to think about how the built environment would function, assuming that: 1) The federal government never fully funded the significant coastal wetland restoration agenda of the day (the Coast 2050 plan); and 2) within the first ten years of that fifty-year horizon a major hurricane hit the city and the levees were breached.

This was a hypothetical scenario at the time. Our plan was to invite leading technical experts to the city to explore future conditions against a range of intervention scenarios. This was an intellectual pursuit grounded in academic and creative practice. We hoped to learn the best approaches. We also very much wanted to scare decision-makers into greater action and preparedness so that we would never need to navigate such a colossal mess. Our funding for this work was secured two weeks before Hurricane Katrina made landfall.

Sitting in Houston in the weeks after Katrina, having established the whereabouts of my primary colleagues working on this (Alan Lewis from TSA and Kevin McCaffrey from ePrime), it became clear what we needed to do. The hypothetical component of our proposal had been obliterated. We contacted our program officer at the Fannie Mae Foundation and received approval to proceed with a more urgent and reconsidered exploration of the future of New Orleans. This new approach would focus on establishing a baseline for the significant planning and reconstruction activities that were to come over the following years. That baseline was to be a set of values and strategies for the future of our city. And it was to be driven by the lived experience of New Orleans residents, who were supported by the relevant technical expertise needed to navigate the immense challenges in front of us.

Over two days in November 2005, we hosted Reinhabiting NOLA at Loyola University in New Orleans. We were not the first group to host a planning meeting during that time, but we were the first to do so with a significant majority of local residents, specifically privileging local knowledge as the driving form of expertise. In that time, we heard from subject matter experts who gave formal presentations of relevant precedent work and methods for approaching planning and rebuilding. We then handed the microphone to a series of community leaders who led group tours through the city–still very sparsely inhabited and full of debris–to describe what it was like to live in this place, the innovations they had developed over generations, and their hopes and fears for what a reconstruction agenda might bring. The symposium finished with passionate discussion amongst small working groups to develop the content of our final report, which we offered as a guide for approaching the city's reconstruction.

That guide had the photo of all participants equal in size and setting on the front cover to demonstrate our clear aim of bringing as many of the right people together and seeing all their knowledge as a form of expertise critical for our situation.

The report did its job of summarizing discussions and presenting specific ways forward. It was formally submitted to the centers of power and resources at that time and was referenced during more formal and empowered planning exercises that were to come. The event seeded many future collaborations, its impact significant but hard to quantify. I think it's best to reference the report directly to summarize the intent and to link it back to the core values of Small Center:

> The basic idea was simple: to pool a diversity of expertise and experience to enact a culturally and environmentally appropriate vision for the long-term recovery of New Orleans neighborhoods and communities. Linking technical knowledge with the expertise of living in the city, the two-day workshop generated an important set of priorities that are grounded in social and environmental justice, as well as good design. At the core of the workshop is the belief that the residents of New Orleans bring essential knowledge to the table.

In Reed Krokoff's closing remarks at Reinhabiting NOLA, he announced that he would be working with me and Alan Lewis to take the priorities articulated at the symposium and use them as the basis on which to launch a design center. While he was correct in that statement, I think what has been more true and more enduring is the framework of values and way of working that drove those two days. From day one, the work of the Center understood lived experience of place as the driving form of expertise necessary to produce exceptional and impactful design and make places and spaces that serve the needs of all people.

Collaborative Efforts

Scott Bernhard

The former Small Center Director reflects on how multiple organizations and initiatives were leveraged to realize Grow Dat Youth Farm.

Our project for an urban agriculture and education facility in New Orleans City Park was a true demonstration of the potential of Small Center. The Grow Dat Youth Farm gathered expertise, relationships across the city, and lessons learned from more than a dozen previous projects to produce an enduring whole much greater than the sum of its parts.

Though architecture can sometimes seem a cumbersome mechanism with which to address social problems, the design and construction of an urban agriculture facility has truly become an instance of design as a tool for positive and measurable social change. The final project demonstrates the capacity of architecture to merge a broad range of concerns and solutions into a single, salient entity–the visible symbol of positive change.

Our Center (then known as the Tulane City Center) drew upon the resources of Tulane University as well as many carefully developed community partnerships to

create a new nonprofit organization and, simultaneously, the facility to support the operation of that nonprofit. Though the farm buildings and the repurposed park landscape are easily associated with the work of architects, landscape architects, and engineers, the hand-in-glove creation of a self-supporting, nonprofit service organization dedicated to addressing several social ills has a less obvious relationship to architecture centers as conventionally understood.

Following a suggestion from Tulane University President Scott Cowen in the Fall of 2010, the Small Center undertook the creation of a new nonprofit that came to be called the "Grow Dat Youth Farm," using elements of the university administration and expertise from across many academic disciplines. At the time, the Small Center consisted of Associate Director and ecologist Dan Etheridge, Design-Build Manager and architect Emilie Taylor Welty, and me, as the Center Director and architect-of-record.

To begin this undertaking, we first renewed a partnership with an experienced health and leadership educator who specialized in work with high-school-age students from diverse backgrounds and neighborhoods. That talented educator, Johanna Gilligan, also had extensive experience with urban farming through her work with the New Orleans Food and Farm Network (another former collaborator of Small Center). She thus became the leader of the youth farm program development which would operate under the umbrella of Tulane University until the new nonprofit she developed could be sufficiently established to stand on its own. Tulane University contributed the talents of development officers and grants administrators to the effort, with all the funds generated to establish the program passed directly to the program itself. This made the process of financial management much easier and was enormously reassuring to grantors and donors who knew that they could trust the university to manage the gifts and grants professionally.

With these elements in place, we produced a "visioning document" with an outline of the youth farm program and the facility that would be constructed to support the farm. The architectural elements of the vision helped to make the proposed program seem real and rooted–something many prospective donors were eager to understand when considering support for a start-up program. The vision also brought another essential partner to the table in the form of New Orleans City Park, which offered four-acres for the youth farm on the site of an abandoned golf course not used since the floods of 2005. Importantly, our partners at New Orleans City Park sought a way to utilize an undesirable portion of the park adjacent to an interstate highway that bisected the park in the 1970s and a surface street built adjacent to the highway. The design task was to make this disused area newly useful and, whenever possible, to make the site more "park-like" and simultaneously put the agricultural activity on display in a fashion appropriate to an urban park. A beautiful stand of mature bald cypress trees already existed on the site and the architecture adopted a position very near but just behind these trees. Careful site grading and even more careful foundation work allowed the cypress trees to ultimately play a major role in water sequestration, bio-filtration, and sun-shading for the farm facility.

The Challenge

As our partners in the School of Public Health and Tropical Medicine explained, two of the most conspicuous problems for young adults in New Orleans–poor health and chronic unemployment–show correlations. Thus, we reasoned that simultaneously addressing both problems could produce results across a range of metrics–from improvements in long-term health and personal agency to the essential skills that support meaningful employment. From the outset, we noted: (1) In 2011, the Bureau of Labor Statistics reported a 42.1 percent rate of unemployment among Black teenagers between ages sixteen and nineteen; and (2) food access studies confirmed that New Orleans was one of the largest urban food deserts in the U.S. with ten supermarkets serving 340,000 people.

These statistics indicated a domino effect, which our team understood as follows. Many New Orleans families did not have regular access to a car and could not reach the few supermarkets near their neighborhoods, leading to inadequate access to healthy food, particularly fresh produce. Many of these same families in the city relied on teenage members to prepare food for the whole family. New Orleans presented very few job opportunities for teenagers and most of what was available was in the fast-food industry. This meant that high-school-aged students often relied on fast-food options to address daily meals, which contributed to chronic health conditions such as diabetes and obesity. Our efforts to address these issues led to funding from a major health insurance company, who believed that supporting our program was a measurable way to improve health outcomes.

Proposal

The Grow Dat Youth Farm seeks to nurture a diverse group of young leaders through the meaningful work of growing food.

Above is the clear and simply stated mission of the youth farm program. Each year, a group of thirty students is selected from area high schools to participate. Students attend workshops, take classes, and participate in extensive leadership training in the after-school program. Each year, students in the program grow 30,000-to-50,000 pounds of sustainably grown, organic produce, selling sixty percent and donating forty percent of the product. Students are paid a stipend, and the sale of the produce forms a significant portion of their compensation. Students are also actively engaged in the distribution of the forty percent of the produce that is donated, making them "ambassadors" of healthy food in their communities.

The ability to achieve our ambition to address these particular social problems was contingent on an inventory of previous successful community and university partnerships. We relied extensively on the lessons we had gathered from earlier, smaller projects with the same partners that we were serving in this new effort. Those relationships had established reasonable expectations, integrated expertise, and, most importantly, trust among the various partners and project advocates.

Most notably, the participation of the Tulane University Social Entrepreneurship Initiative, the Tulane Office of the President, the Tulane School of Medicine's community health initiative, the Cowen Institute for Public Education Initiatives, and the Tulane University Office of Advancement were crucial elements of the initiative. In the community beyond the university, we worked with the New Orleans Food and Farm Network, New Orleans City Park, Clean Plate Enterprises, Engineers Without Borders, the Hollygrove Growers Farm and Market, and more than a dozen other nonprofit groups and expert associations. Each of these organizations was willing to take risks to participate in the project, and each made generous donations of time and expertise to the effort. More than a dozen granting organizations supported the work, including a major corporation and generous support from individual donors.

Gathering Partners and Insight in a Pilot Year

Once the operational concept of the Youth Farm had been established and the core personnel had been engaged, preliminary funding for a pilot year of the program was secured. The goal of the pilot year was to develop insight into the physical requirements of the program and to examine the relationship between the architectural setting and the needs, both practical and poetic, of the program participants. The permanent facility was developed during the pilot year. Landscape architect Abigail Feldman and I led two initial design studios, producing complete design and construction drawings for the urban farming facility and four-acre agricultural site. Each of these design studios regularly asked for input from the high school students in the pilot program. Anticipating a subsequent design-build project, Small Center Design-Build Manager Emilie Taylor Welty joined us frequently to advise and plan the segue to construction.

One small example of a programmatic/spatial insight from the pilot year had to do with the daily process of high school students changing shoes to work on the muddy agricultural tasks. The pilot program facility did not offer many places to sit comfortably to change from school shoes to farm shoes. This resulted in twenty minutes of every class session being devoted to the simple task of donning appropriate

// ABOVE: Grow Dat's indoor/outdoor mezzanine spaces. Photo by Will Crocker.

footwear. Similarly, a convenient and secure place to store "clean" shoes was not available and many minutes were wasted in trying to situate student belongings. In the final design of the permanent facility, the designers were careful to position a broad flight of low, wide steps immediately in front of the locker/storage room and between the outdoor classroom and the path to the agricultural fields. Students would move through "clean zones" or "dry zones" in the classroom and courtyard spaces of the project, then pass though the carefully designed transition spaces to change shoes, store backpacks, and gather tools on the way to the fields, and again to return tools and clean-up on the way back to the classroom at the end of the day. Many design concepts emerged in this way.

With Thanks

Our partners within Tulane and amidst the New Orleans community have always been fundamental to the work of Small Center, as the plethora of contributors described above indicates. The Farm solved a problem in City Park by activating an unused space with a revenue-producing and community-building facility aimed at addressing pernicious social ills. It was truly a notable synergy. The twenty-one organizations and departments mentioned in this summary, the sixty-one architecture students, the fifteen high school students of the pilot year, the seven School of Architecture faculty, and the many donating sub-contractors and volunteers are too numerous to itemize here. Joined in a common effort, these people and organizations created a visible symbol of hope and ambition in New Orleans–one that continues today, more than a decade along.

Welcoming Community

Suzanne-Juliette Mobley

The former Small Center Public Programs Manager provides examples of how gathering in conversation and connecting across disciplines can produce real changes, and the importance of building an audience outside of the Center's institution helps build trust over time.

Small Center moved from Tulane's campus to Central City in August of 2014, gaining (amongst many other things) a big, open, extremely empty storefront space at 1725 Baronne. For four years, it was my responsibility to creatively fill that space, and to do so in the spirit of Small Center's efforts from the beginning, namely gathering across sectors, facilitating critical conversations, and constituency-building. To that end, we hosted conferences and charrettes for national funders, neighborhood activists, and municipal agencies. We developed exhibits out of collaborations and design projects, which in turn created new collaborations, new projects, and new exhibits. We convened panel discussions about the big issues impacting our little

city, opening the Center to the public for monthly evenings of casual dinner and serious conversations. Along the way, we helped to build a diverse, interdisciplinary, and energized community of people whose curiosity shaped our work in return and for the better.

Maybe it was the moment, or the money, but for New Orleans, Fall of 2014 was an inflection point. Mitch Landrieu's election to a second term as mayor solidified an entrepreneurial approach to recovery, and concerns about gentrification and displacement were intensifying rapidly. New Orleans was riding a wave of public investment unparalleled since the early days of federal urban aid, a massive influx of philanthropic giving just shifting from immediate disaster recovery to longer-term revitalization and private investment spurred by hosting the 2013 Super Bowl. A deluge of outside do-gooders and policy wonks, layered atop the city's markedly racialized, inequitable recovery, caused the city to pivot towards insularity. In conversation after conversation, there was a sense that New Orleans was at a crossroads with a real risk (or hope, depending on your perspective,) that the city's future would be determined by temporary people making permanent decisions.

Small Center's team planted ourselves firmly at that crossroads. Or maybe the move to the center of the city brought home the intersections at which we already stood. Organizationally, we had done a decade of work building networks with community partners, government agencies, and design collaborators that reached across the city and the country. As a group of people whose roots in the city ranged from generational to newly arrived, and whose professional fields varied as well, we were acutely aware that our professional and personal diversity was an asset, and that our contributions were sharpest when our different perspectives were fully integrated. We were also pretty cognizant that the process of engaging, even amongst our team, wasn't always smooth. It takes a tremendous amount of work and trust, a willingness to learn, and a belief in each other's fundamental good intentions to collaborate across differences.

So, when we set out to create a welcoming space for everyone to shape the place we call home, we were also drawing on the ongoing labor of building cohesion with each other and bringing the complicated process of community-making out into the public and up onto the exhibition walls. We both learned and modeled how to deliberately build across differences, leveraging our varied networks to connect across sectors and social barriers. We explicitly softened the boundaries between expert and audience to facilitate conversations where we could all learn and teach together. We created opportunities for people to connect casually and consistently, with an open-door policy for attendance at structured teach-ins on complex policy issues, along with unstructured drop-ins from neighbors wanting to chat about street flooding or public sector colleagues looking for cupcakes.

We developed accessible exhibits and designed tools for shared understanding: breaking down, for example, the complexities of housing policy and histories of public investment, and putting those in conversation with the stories of families just trying to keep a roof over their heads. Each of these approaches was part of making visible and knowable the natural, built, and social environments that layer together to make up New Orleans. We especially prioritized the specificity of the local, or even hyperlocal, explorations of issues that are fundamentally national, historic, and cultural. Each of these approaches was part of building cohesion at a pivotal moment, when the city had the chance to redesign our places and policies to correct problematic legacies, restore justice, and sustain our collective lives.

The urgency has only increased in the years since, and, with it, both the need for, and challenges to, creating spaces and constituencies that can chart a path forward and design a more just future. We will have to learn new ways to learn from each other to meet and solve those challenges because the world we need depends on our exchange of information, expertise, tactics, stories, and truths. If we can't understand all of the parts of our collective puzzle, from the path dependency created by generations of policy choices, to where the power to make decisions lies, or where opportunities for coalition exist, then we cannot build a cohesive community that can face the challenges ahead. We can't solve problems unless we commit to learning the contexts in which those problems exist and the conditions under which they arose. This sounds simple, but real learning is fundamentally uncomfortable, and many of us, perhaps most of us, really dislike being uncomfortable.

That discomfort is never more apparent than when we are learning across the distances created by legacies of slavery and segregation, disparate understandings of our shared histories, and wild differentials in power and poverty. To build across these differences requires that we know each other by face and by name, and that we build trust for the hard work of learning together. Enough trust to believe someone's story even when it sounds different than the narrative we were taught, enough trust to believe someone's good intentions can be met with critique without prompting a catastrophe, and ultimately enough trust in each other and ourselves to be willing to ask questions, make mistakes, and make amends.

2

Recovering Stories of Place

"Designs informed by a knowledge of everyday life contribute to the protection of cultural practices and create a city alive with creative expression."

The stories we tell about our city and its history inform how we imagine its future. Collective storytelling is a powerful tool for highlighting the rhythms of everyday life and the ways that cultural practices continue to hold and shape space. As a tool to inform design and policy conversations, storytelling centers the expertise of lived experience and foregrounds the value of spaces that house cultural traditions. Storytelling practices are used at the start of a project to set expectations and then throughout Small Center's community engagement process as a research method. Small Center understands the development of design projects to be part of the collective weaving of a story of place. This story is informed by complex histories, grounded by present circumstances, and defines a vision of the future. After a project is selected, the project partner and Small Center's team work through a series of questions to determine the project's expectations and scope. In many ways, this conversation serves as a first pass of the overall "story" of the project.

What is the primary goal of the project? How will this project's success be measured?

These questions shed light on participants' assumptions and set expectations before the project begins. The Center brings architectural skills to the projects it takes on, but not every project requires an architecturally designed and built structure. By situating each project within the short-term and long-range strategic goals of the partner organization, this pre-design conversation aims to avoid creating beautiful but unnecessary structures that are costly to maintain and do not advance the organization's ability to serve its constituents.

Who are the stakeholders in this project, and what are the most effective methods for engagement? How can engagement activities help build capacity within the communities served?

This next series of questions informs engagement strategies. Each partner is different. Some organizations have extensive experience in engagement practices, and Small Center can work with their existing feedback systems. For other organizations, these questions open new opportunities to develop engagement methods. Engagement flows naturally from design projects, which offer a reason to talk with a variety of groups about the future of the city, the future role of the organization, and the strategic path towards realizing these visions. Small Center facilitates these design discussions between potential funders, strategic partners, and allies, and offers new perspectives, advice, and resources, strengthening and expanding each partner's network of supporters.

What are the student learning objectives? Are there readings the partner organization recommends to better understand its work and the communities it serves?

Given Small Center's position within an academic institution, students' learning opportunities are critical. Indeed, the question of student learning provides a chance to reinforce the position of community partners as experts in the process, not passive recipients of aid. The exchange of knowledge is reciprocal with the students lending design expertise and the partner organization informing student designers about the organization's mission and the communities it serves. Sometimes this means reading a few key articles. At other times, this includes other cultural artifacts: music, movies, or tours of similar sites in the city. Often, it requires students to spend time as "participant-observers," volunteering with the organization to understand the people it serves, the people who work there, and their needs.

How does the project educate the public and expand knowledge about key issues for New Orleans residents? At the project's conclusion, how will the project be celebrated?

The final set of questions looks ahead to imagine the project's completion as a turning point for the partner organization, transitioning it into the next chapter of work. In preparation for this final stage, Small Center builds relationships with strategic allies and offers advocacy tools to the organization. Advocacy on complex issues is an ongoing process, so the Center remains available to support organizations as they build public understanding of the issues at the core of their work.

At the conclusion of Small Center's design work, the project's final celebration reminds everyone involved to take a break to reflect. It also offers an event where allies and decision-makers can attend and become part of the project's support network. By discussing the project's conclusion during the initial visioning conversations, the Center sets the stage for ongoing discussions about the expertise needed to inform the project. To the extent possible, students are invited to join these conversations. Thoughtful collaboration and strategic coalition building are both skills that take time, care, and consistent, intentional communication. While the design process supports conversations about the past, present, and future of a place and an organization, the structure of the space and time for the conversation itself is also designed.

A variety of cultural influences and practices have shaped New Orleans. These histories deserve to be recognized, preserved, and understood as significant contributions to New Orleans culture. However, narratives about the architectural fabric tend to focus on the influence of European ideas and the contributions of singular, white men. Small Center uses storytelling to complicate these narratives. The city's built environment has been profoundly shaped by the work of residents, often marginalized groups, to claim space for their own cultural life and survival.

Under French, Spanish, and Antebellum American rule, the region was shaped by enslaved laborers who constructed levees and drained and filled the swamps

and bayous. Individuals escaping slavery formed "Maroon" communities in the surrounding bayous and applied their land management and food cultivation skills to survival as an autonomous, communal society, learning from, and collaborating with, indigenous tribes.[24] They recognized their entanglement with the environment and cared for the land through shared stewardship practices. Recent efforts to restore the wetland ecosystem echo their strategies for self-determination.

Within the city, the use of public space has a similarly subversive history. The city's culture of joyfully claiming space with parades, music, festivals, and spectacle also traces its roots back to political acts. "Social aid and pleasure clubs," or mutual aid societies, filled gaps in social support services for Black residents, and later for immigrant communities, by offering members access to medical services and pensions, as well as social events. "Second lines" and "jazz funerals" emerged from these organizations. In both cases, marching with the brass band offered protected access to the city, representing resistance to policies of segregation and the economic forces causing displacement. The second line in particular brought this culture across the city for the public to experience free of charge.[25] Second lines continue to function as both mobile public squares and Sunday forums, open to those willing to move with the band.[26]

As these narratives, which complicate the mainstream focus on New Orleans's colonial influences, show, place can be a window into lesser-known histories. Small Center recognizes the importance of preserving sites that symbolize collective histories and support the cultural activities of the many different communities that animate the city. This belief underpins the Center's selection of projects, as it seeks those shaped by community leadership and prioritizing historically marginalized groups. Small Center documents the significance of sites that hold space for music, craft, and the exchange of traditions across generations. The Center documents these activities and their home spaces in its exhibitions, so that people can understand other cultures without appropriating them.

The projects in this chapter recover stories of everyday life that are often marginalized in the grand narrative of New Orleans history. By collecting and documenting these narratives in the design process, the Center aims to illustrate the significance of everyday life and individual neighborhoods in the city's culture. Designs informed by practical, everyday use contribute to the protection of cultural practices, create a city alive with creative expression, and reinforce residents' sense of belonging.

This chapter highlights projects in which storytelling is used as a tool for humanizing policy discussions. Images and narratives illustrate the impacts of public policies on the lives of specific residents. The Center hopes that these illustrations move conversations about design, economics, and policies past abstract data and toward the tangible quality of life experienced by real people.

---

[24] Diane J. Allen, "Living Freedom Through the Maroon Landscape," *Places Journal* (2022). https://doi.org/10.22269/220922.

[25] George Lipsitz, *How Racism Takes Place* (Temple University Press, 2011).

[26] Joel Dinerstein, "Second Lining Post-Katrina: Learning Community from the Prince of Wales Social Aid and Pleasure Club," *American Quarterly* 61, no. 3 (2009): 615-637.

VISIONING

Façade RENEW

Revitalizing Locally Owned Historic Storefronts, 2013 - 2016

In January 2013, Small Center partnered with the New Orleans Redevelopment Authority (NORA) to create a grant program for redeveloping historic commercial corridors in New Orleans. Small Center worked with NORA to identify pilot sites for targeted investment, prioritizing historic commercial corridors with locally owned businesses and active storefronts. NORA recognized the importance of commercial revitalization as a tool for rebuilding New Orleans into a city of walkable neighborhoods with locally-owned small businesses. The program supported improvements for small businesses that otherwise might not have been able to afford to restore their facades.

The two-year pilot targeted portions of three corridors: Bayou Road, St. Claude Avenue, and Oretha Castle Haley Boulevard. In addition, placemaking grants supported initiatives along Alcee Fortier Boulevard in New Orleans East and at the

// ABOVE: Before & after photos of a building that was renovated under Façade Renew
// PREVIOUS: Cafe Reconcile was a notable participant in the program.

intersection of Oretha Castle Haley Boulevard and Martin Luther King Jr. Boulevard in Central City. Each corridor was facing specific threats to historic architecture and unique challenges for small businesses. Bayou Road is the oldest road in New Orleans and home to a concentration of Black women business owners facing significant pressures from gentrification. Research confirmed the street's long history as a site of trade and façade improvements supported the street's Afro-Caribbean identity. Oretha Castle Haley Boulevard was the site of significant Civil Rights actions and has become home to multiple cultural institutions. Historic preservation efforts offered a chance to call attention to the national significance of the street as the site of the Dryades Street Boycott, while investing in its revitalization. These investments included renovating a plaza at the corner of Martin Luther King Jr. Boulevard, centered on the installation of a sculpture by internationally recognized artist, Frank Hayden. St. Claude Avenue had already emerged as an arts district, but its designation as a state highway limited opportunities for signage and public space interventions. Alcee Fortier Boulevard connected the heart of a neighborhood in New Orleans East known for its community farm, weekly farmers market, and the history of community organizing through Mary Queen of Vietnam Church. Placemaking efforts along the Boulevard aimed to celebrate the community's food traditions while welcoming new residents who brought cultural traditions from Latin America and elsewhere.

The program offered façade improvement grants for individual building owners and placemaking grants to main street associations. Small Center provided technical design assistance for each of the grant applicants to prepare historic research and design documents necessary for municipal approval. In addition to efficiently administering the program for storefront participants, the Center offered students an opportunity to work with a preservation architect. Resulting designs were informed by careful archival research into the historic and cultural heritage of particular properties, ensuring the standards of historic preservation were upheld. Focused research into the histories of the buildings revealed life along these main streets at different moments in the city's history. Many business owners delighted in the opportunity to learn about their building's history while maintaining it. Storefront rehabilitation included painting, exterior repairs, lighting, and signage.

The two-year pilot program included an investment of over $1.5 million toward the revitalization of these commercial corridors. The program surpassed its participation goals and subsequent funding has supported façade improvements on other historic commercial corridors in the city. The preservation architecture research for Oretha Castle Haley Boulevard formed the basis of the first official exhibit in Small Center's Baronne Street gallery space, one block south.

Dew Drop Inn

Restoring an Historic Performance Venue, 2014

The Dew Drop Inn is one of the most significant music heritage sites in New Orleans. Started as a barbershop and refreshment stand on LaSalle Street, the business expanded into a bar, a hotel, and eventually a dancehall and restaurant. The venue presented comedians, musicians, dancers, drag queens, and other performers, and hosted many legends of rock and roll early in their careers: Little Richard, Irma Thomas, and Ray Charles, among other local and national talents. Operating during segregation, it offered Black visitors a good meal, a safe hotel, a haircut, and entertainment.[27] Serving as a hangout for musicians between gigs, visitors often enjoyed lively, after-hours jam sessions.

The performance venue closed around 1970 and the business was shuttered entirely following damage from Hurricane Katrina in 2005. In 2010, it was recognized with Historic Landmark status and listed as an endangered New Orleans historic site by the Louisiana Landmarks Society. Its original owners, the Painia family, hoped to

revitalize it as a neighborhood institution and bring music back to LaSalle Street in Central City.

Previous research on the Dew Drop Inn's cultural significance, developed by Tulane's Historic Preservation program, informed Small Center's study of the Inn's revitalization. Small Center created architectural plans that recovered the original mixed use as a hotel, restaurant, barber shop, and music venue, alongside new programming to support youth in the arts. A strategic partnership between the Painia Family, the Milne Inspiration Center, and Harmony Neighborhood Development supported these efforts to save the historic cultural center and return it to use.

To bring attention to the Dew Drop Inn's significance and the restoration effort, Small Center constructed and installed a temporary façade across the building, featuring pictures of some of the Inn's historic performers. Images of the temporary façade in local media helped amplify the effort.

Though Small Center's organizing, capacity building, and design visioning processes seeded the fundraising campaign for, and public awareness of, the Dew Drop Inn, progress took years. Following a decade of starts and stops, in 2024, the Dew Drop Inn reopened after a dynamic renovation effort led by local developer Curtis Doucette, Jr., the legendary, historically significant club made available to the public once more.

[27] Hannah Chalew and Al Jackson, "Dew Drop Inn," *New Orleans Historical*, June 5, 2018, https://neworleanshistorical.org/items/show/1432.

EXHIBIT

The Cost of Home

Local Models and National Policy for Affordability, 2016

Following Small Center's move to a neighborhood-based location, the Center experimented with different ways that the "storefront" gallery space could support and inform ongoing design work and policy conversations. The exhibit space offered an opportunity to humanize these conversations through stories of real-life impacts. As described in Chapter 1, *The Cost of Home* exhibit piloted a model for highlighting the work of past projects, partners, and local organizations working on critical issues in the city. The exhibit examined the national and local landscape of affordable housing by visualizing the programs, policies, and design politics that have shaped, and continue to shape, New Orleans and the nation. The exhibit drew from nearly ten years of the Center's work addressing affordable housing using a variety of approaches, including research in and outside of the city. The studies included critical reflection on the Center's work in partnership with Jane Place Neighborhood Sustainability Initiative, Jericho Road, Greater New Orleans Fair Housing Action Center, and Greater New Orleans Housing Alliance. Through images and narrative

text, *The Cost of Home* presented case studies that contextualized the current models of design and programming that provide housing for low- to moderate-income residents in New Orleans. Case studies from other cities demonstrated the potential of underutilized alternatives.

In addition to typical design exhibit materials illustrating physical forms and policy frameworks, the exhibit aimed to represent the impacts of the housing market on the lives of residents through a series of visual stories. Developed in collaboration with local artist Justin Shiels, the stories depicted New Orleans families at different income brackets as they navigated the tradeoffs in local housing choices. These narratives brought cost burdens out of abstract numbers and provided relatable examples of how issues of housing affordability play out. A coordinated series of panel discussions offered an opportunity for the public to ask questions of policymakers, developers, and housing advocates. The conversation extended to national leaders when the exhibit traveled for display at the Fannie Mae Headquarters in Washington, D.C.

.

BUILD

Guardians Institute

The Donald Harrison Sr. Cultural Museum and Legacy Performance Pavilion, 2011 - 2012

In 2006, Herreast J. Harrison founded the Guardians Institute in honor of her late husband, Big Mardi Gras Indian Chief, Donald Harrison, Sr. (1933-1998). As a child, Mr. Harrison followed the Uptown neighborhood Indian tribes, learning the traditions, dances, and skills of beading, and began masking for Carnival in 1949. He was a former Big Chief of the Creole Wild West, Cherokee Braves, and White Eagles tribes before founding the Guardians of the Flame in 1988. Harrison studied and drew inspiration from the ceremonial traditions of Native American tribes and the arts of West Africa and frequently spoke about Mardi Gras Indian culture to a variety of audiences.[28] The Institute continues this work and plays a vital role in preserving cultural arts unique to New Orleans. By providing space and programming for culture-bearers to disseminate their knowledge directly to the next generation, they help to ensure the practices are not lost or altered. Since its founding, the Guardians Institute has also been dedicated to supporting young people through

literacy, cultural arts, and West African and New World oral traditions. Small Center partnered with the Guardians Institute to build a small performance, education, and storage space for use by the Institute and the Guardians of the Flame Mardi Gras Indian Tribe. The Institute hosts workshops on sewing, jazz, art, and a book club, as well as public events.

The design of the Institute references the local architecture, reimagined as a space for performance and gathering. The building is proportioned like a shotgun house, yet oriented parallel to the street to position the porch as a stage. Set back within a double lot to offer ample yard space for community gathering, its height and breadth are informed by the size of a fully "masked" chief. The stage and the oversized stairs become seating for a captive audience. Behind a double-layered surface of white polygal is a space primarily used for the well-established literacy program and other teaching endeavors of the Institute.

The structure was designed and constructed through multiple Tulane studios and was intended for short term use. The Institute demonstrates the potential for a much grander museum space in the future, by housing and displaying artwork, music collections, and many other artifacts from the Harrisons, as well as other artists. The Guardians Institute has curated dozens of exhibits, seminars, lectures, and presentations in New Orleans and throughout the world. The space is significant in supporting the Guardians of the Flame in maintaining control of their own culture and cultural artifacts, such as photos, music, and traditional suits.

[28]"New Orleans Spirit: The Donald Harrison, Sr. Family Papers," *Amistad Research Center Blog*, February 20, 2018, https://www.amistadresearchcenter.org/single-post/2018/02/20/new-orleans-spirit-the-donald-harrison-sr-family-papers.

VISIONING

Hung Dao Heritage Gardens

A Park Preserving Vietnamese Cultural Traditions, 2013 - 2014

Established in the 1970s by refugees from the Vietnam War, New Orleans' Vietnamese communities represent some of the strongest ethnic cultures in the region. A Catholic city with a subtropical climate and lowland topography, New Orleans offered an opportunity for a life similar to Vietnam. In Lower Algiers, the Hung Dao community has grown to approximately 350 families. The community recognizes the importance of passing down its cultural traditions to the next generations. The Hung Dao Gardens are imagined as a heritage park that will tell the story of the community through plantings, food, and traditions native to all regions of Vietnam.

Small Center worked with the Louisiana State University Landscape Lab and the Hung Dao Community Development Corporation to create a plan for the heritage garden and pursue realizing that vision. Leaders in the community identified a

blighted 6.5-acre site. They worked with local councilmember Kristin Palmer and the Louisiana Land Trust to demolish the abandoned apartment complex on the site and transfer the land to the community for the proposed park. The Hung Dao community established a community development corporation to acquire ownership of the land and forge relationships with key partners.

Small Center held a series of community meetings to inform design plans. The resulting park plan includes a cultural center, new sports fields, and landscaped gardens. In addition to these new public spaces, the design addresses local flooding through green infrastructure and drainage improvements. The park design creates a place for locals and visitors to engage with Hung Dao's Vietnamese culture through youth education, gardening and food cultivation, recreation, sports, and cultural events. The park will host the community's famous Vietnamese New Year's celebration, or Tet festival, which includes symbolic food, music, dance, and crafts.

The park proposal formed the basis for multiple funding applications, and, in 2023, support was secured to realize the design. The project received funding from the Greater New Orleans Foundation for the "Resilient Algiers Project," through a collaboration with the Song Community Development Corporation, a nonprofit working on climate resilience in New Orleans East, and the New Orleans Hazard Mitigation Office. The realization of this project, led by local residents, will preserve and celebrate Vietnamese cultural traditions for future generations, while contributing to the neighborhood's well-being by reducing local stormwater.

EXHIBIT

Legacy of Central City

Celebrating Neighborhood History and Culture, 2022

When Small Center moved to the Baronne Street location, the first exhibit centered on the history of Oretha Castle Haley Boulevard in Central City. Research for the exhibit was drawn from Small Center's preservation and restoration work along the Boulevard through Façade RENEW and was curated by Small Center's design team. *Legacy of Central City* expanded on the narratives of the neighborhood by showcasing the work of Central City-based artists and culture-bearers, alongside research, and a series of public events. The local nonprofit, Civic Studio, curated the exhibit and coordinated public programs in Small Center's storefront gallery.

The exhibit traced the transformation of a watery backswamp into a working-class neighborhood. Central City's history and culture can be traced back to the cypress swamps of *Bulbancha*, the indigenous name for the area in which New Orleans is now found. In Choctaw and Chickasaw, it means "place of many tongues," emphasizing the region's long history as a place of exchange. Large, wall-sized drawings, collages, and a mural spoke to different eras in the neighborhood's development, emphasizing the relationship between place and cultural production. The neighborhood has fostered social aid and pleasure clubs, brass band and Mardi Gras Indian traditions, and the

founding of the Southern Christian Leadership Conference and the New Orleans chapter of the Congress of Racial Equity. Exhibit images identified the roots of Civil Rights era activism in connection to neighborhood parks, streets, and churches. Maps and diagrams described the preservation and loss of these neighborhood centers over time. Other artwork and artifacts revealed how some of hip hop's major hits provide insights into life in public housing and offer a glimpse into what New Orleans was like before the impact of Hurricane Katrina.

The exhibit aimed to inspire local young people through an understanding of neighborhood history. Interactive workshops and events provided opportunities to engage the social, cultural, and environmental histories of the neighborhood. One of Big Chief Beautiful's intricately crafted Black Masking Indian suits held a prominent wall, and beading instruction sessions demonstrated the techniques. Work by photographer Polo Silk, writer Sharita Sims, and artists Brianna Brady, Aron Chang, and others highlighted Central City's legacy of creative expression. A book launch event for Melpomene Street Blues included food and live music, as well as a chance to explore of artifacts recovered from the site of homes demolished in the 1960s to build the William J. Guste Sr. Homes, or "the Melph." A series of walking tours highlighted neighborhood landmarks with local guides. Hands-on workshops included local gardener Jeanette Bell teaching students how to harvest mulberries and plant radishes, and opportunities to plant rain gardens to shape a new relationship with water. These activities demonstrated how the local history of activism and creative production continues in the work of the many artists, nonprofit leaders, and culture-bearers who live and work in Central City.

Channeling Small Center

Maurice Cox

The former Small Center Director shares the experience of serial engagement along the Lasalle Cultural Corridor in the Center's neighborhood of Central City, and the importance of helping create spaces for culture-bearers to share their work through public gathering. Adapted from a live presentation at AIA New Orleans, March 3, 2024.

I am a lover of cities. At times, my career has focused on those areas that are understood to be the heart of cities: the downtowns, the waterfronts, and the places that belong to everyone. But from the work that I've done with communities, I understand that there's also a soul of a city, and that soul resides in neighborhoods. Neighborhoods are the laboratory for innovation. While I have spent time in both the heart and soul of cities, the work that I've felt most called to do is to give attention to the soul.

My journey started as an organizer in Charlottesville, Virginia, as president of the Ridge Street Neighborhood Association, which I co-founded with longtime residents. We wanted to advocate for the community we lived in, which was ninety-eight percent African American and a beautiful neighborhood recognized as a national historic district, but not protected under any local designation that would prevent structures from being demolished. I started working with my fellow residents, asking pointed questions to political leaders about why our neighborhood was still overlooked. And,

together, we got Ridge Street Historic District recognized locally. It was the first low-income area and the only majority African American neighborhood of Charlottesville to be so designated.

By using the cultural history of Ridge Street to stir the souls of residents into collective action, I began to understand the work of the designer as inherently political, and thus requiring more political power. So, my title changed–from architect to organizer to city councilor to mayor–but no matter what position I took, my purpose was to use planning and design to help communities evolve and tell their own stories. I also began to understand that trying to get people to embrace innovation is really a challenging task. And, in fact, what we're often doing when we ask communities to change is asking them to confront "an adaptive challenge," a term coined by Ronald Heifetz. Success in adaptive work requires new learning on the part of all constituents. The resistance that we find to innovation often has to do with the fact that people don't have the tools to see the gap between their current physical reality and their community values. This understanding has helped me craft some principles that start with the simple notion that every citizen has the right to live in a well-designed community, and that, to be effective, the design process must be a democratic one. You're asking folks to tackle really tough challenges. To do that, you must willingly give that work back to the people who will be affected by it and design according to their values–not your own values or our disciplines' prescribed values.

I had an opportunity to practice this method during my time in New Orleans at Small Center. As a university-community partnership, the Center supports locally-led projects that help communities adapt and change. The Center offers a framework by which faculty and students can contribute to changing the built and natural environments. These projects are guided by the notion of incremental change, helping people build capacity to take on bigger challenges. I also served in the role of Associate Dean of Community Engagement, which came with a specific directive to leverage the real estate program, preservation program, architecture, and other disciplines like landscape architecture (in partnership with Louisiana State University). We brought all of these disciplines to bear on really challenging questions in New Orleans. It was a deeply collaborative way of working that has stayed with me. Later in my career, I built my teams in the cities of Detroit and Chicago with this interdisciplinary approach in mind.

I also worked to integrate New Orleans culture into the core curriculum of the School of Architecture. One of our most unique and meaningful partnerships was our work with the New Orleans Mardi Gras Indian Council (MGIC). The Council represented entrepreneurs and cultural leaders, and hundreds of years of Mardi Gras Indian masking. They were trying to understand their role, post-Hurricane Katrina, in keeping their history and traditions alive, and how their community could become an anchor and driver for economic development. They brought these questions to the Small Center. Imagine the Mardi Gras Indians allowing students to analyze, handle, and reinterpret their suits as a part of their education. The students got enormous benefit out of the exchange, but so did the Mardi Gras Indians. Through our conversations, we discovered that these gentlemen were preservationists—they were preservationists of culture.

As designers, our job was to give them a physical manifestation of how that culture could be housed and displayed. We helped to create the largest video archive of their stories, created a framework for a cultural campus across from their home location of A.L. Davis Park, and supported them in envisioning LaSalle Street as their cultural corridor. The ability for the Mardi Gras Indian Council to guide the direction of an entire street corridor was profound. We hosted "walkshops," which looked like going down the block, identifying properties, and describing what they might become to anchor a cultural district. Our job as facilitators was to help the MGIC understand how to put together a financial proposal that is able to attract investments, and how

to use design as a tool to claim the block as their cultural space. With the help of the Foundation for Louisiana and Art Place America, we secured a $500,000 grant. In February 2020, the Council took possession of two buildings and renovated them as their permanent museum and educational center. Their sculptural, artistic work that had been precariously housed in a multipurpose youth center is now at the center of their own campus. I saw these men become innovators, developers, and–yes–designers, who were able to direct the future of the corridor.

Simultaneously, Byron Mouton and Tulane's URBANbuild program led other work on the corridor that helped spark a transformation. URBANbuild built a Saturday food and artisans market, and, next door, the YAYA Arts Center opened its doors to support arts education for youth. Like charms on a bracelet, incremental interventions began to tie the corridor together.

Down the street, we supported a vision to bring the renowned jazz venue, the Dew Drop Inn, back to life. My talented, beautiful, and amazing wife Giovanna Galfione was the design lead. At the time, we knew this was going to be a heavy lift. All we could do was try to get the building off of the New Orleans blighted properties list and help people understand its phenomenal history. We used a tactical strategy, choosing archival photographs to enlarge on a temporary, printed fabric installation. The building's programmatic outline included a hotel, barbershop, and supper club. It took time, but that program has been realized today by developer Curtis Doucette Jr. From my perspective, La Salle Street's revitalization started with the Mardi Gras Indians claiming it as a cultural corridor. It wasn't a big master plan, but a series of small steps that blossomed and will continue to grow until the physical space finally reflects the rich and vibrant community it serves.

This incremental way of working has stayed with me and permeated my portfolio in both Detroit and Chicago. I've always been interested in how you go beyond simply including people. Small Center offers a model for giving people an ownership stake and allowing them to drive the planning process. Incremental projects, audacious results. I'm channeling Small Center every step of the way, simply taking it to another scale.

More than a City

Melissa Lee

The former Senior Adviser for Commercial Revitalization at New Orleans Redevelopment Authority reflects on the multiple outcomes of refreshing historic storefronts.

New Orleans–what a city. She is a seductress, effortlessly drawing you under her spell. Like any enchantress, she is enticing, bewildering, unpredictable, exciting, scheming, and irresistible: a living paradox. But New Orleans is more than a city; she is a spirit and a culture.

This spirit and culture reside in the historic architecture woven throughout the city's neighborhoods. Each streetscape carries a unique identity reflected in its collections of commercial, residential, religious, and institutional structures. These buildings are more than mere edifices, they are symbols of the city's history and character. They serve as tangible links between the past and present, illustrating how commerce and community thrive in harmony.

In 2013, New Orleans was undergoing a pivotal transformation. Neighborhood-wide commercial development was surging, fueled by public-private investments made in the preceding years. However, a troubling pattern began to emerge: recovery dollars and their benefits often bypassed areas adjacent to well-established commercial

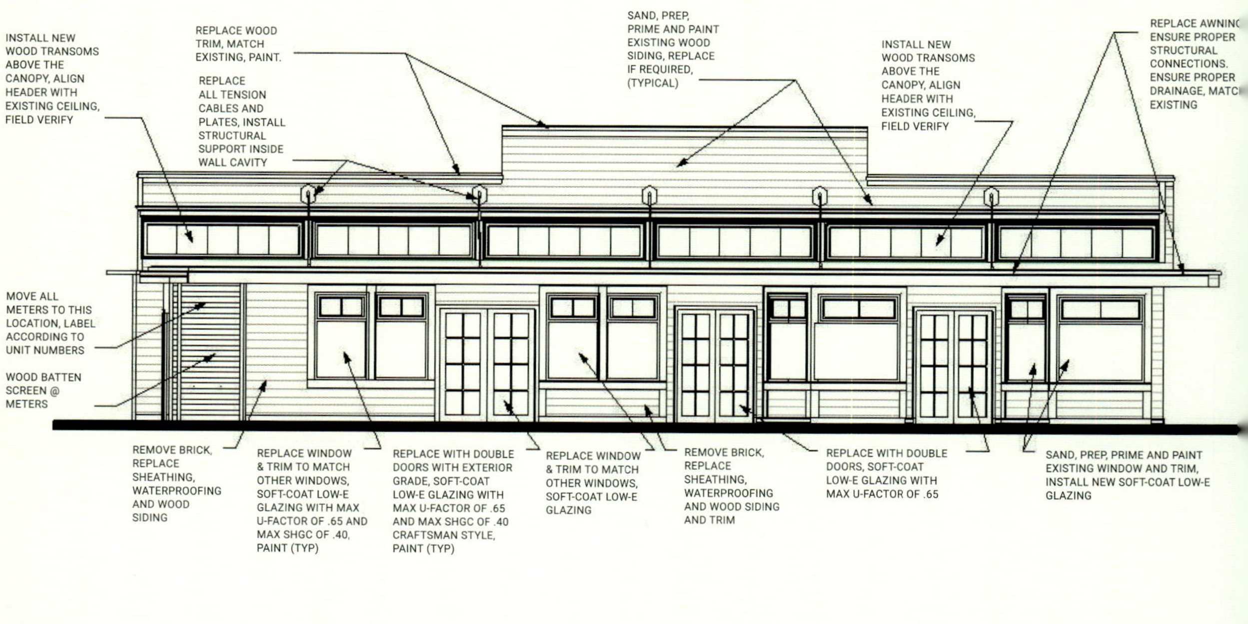

corridors. This raised pressing questions: Does this allocation represent a just city? Why does preservation prioritize some areas over others? How can public-private investments be balanced equitably?

To address these challenges, the New Orleans Redevelopment Authority (NORA) launched Façade RENEW in partnership with Small Center. This initiative targeted commercial corridors like Oretha Castle Haley Boulevard, Bayou Road, and St. Claude Avenue. Façade RENEW operated as a 3:1 reimbursable grant program, incentivizing commercial property and small business owners to revitalize their buildings. The program covered seventy-five percent of façade improvement costs, up to $37,500 per property. In 2015, the initiative expanded to include Old Gentilly Road and Alcee Fortier Boulevard.

Façade RENEW sought to preserve the historical and cultural essence of these corridors while stimulating economic growth. The program conducted extensive research into the heritage of each property, informing a collaborative design process that celebrated the city's layered history. Through this approach, the program unearthed stories of New Orleans's people and places, fostering a deeper appreciation of the past and guiding thoughtful, equitable planning for the future.

Improvements funded by the program ranged from painting, exterior repairs, and lighting, to signage and full storefront rehabilitations. These enhancements encouraged adaptive reuse and introduced new, contextually sensitive design interventions. Clio Associates LLC, in collaboration with Small Center, provided thirty hours of technical design assistance to each grant applicant.

The results were transformative. Façade RENEW invested nearly $2 million in Disaster-Community Development Block Grant (D-CDBG) funds, facilitating approximately forty-five façade improvement projects. This investment leveraged an additional $19.5 million in private investments, leading to the creation of new businesses, local jobs, and strengthened organizational and business infrastructures.

Today, these revitalized commercial corridors retain their historic fabric while serving as catalysts for broader reinvestment in New Orleans' neighborhoods. Perhaps most significantly, the program expanded the benefits of reinvestment to a wider demographic, fostering a more equitable city.

Façade RENEW provides a compelling case study for exploring critical questions: What constitutes a just city? Why do preservation efforts favor some areas over others? And how can public-private investments achieve the right balance? Through initiatives like this, New Orleans demonstrates how to navigate these questions while celebrating her spirit, culture, and enduring allure.

Learning in the Public Interest

Matt Williams

The former Small Center Design Fellow reflects on learning the tools of engagement while working with the Mardi Gras Indian Council.

I was in my second year of graduate school at Louisiana State University, and I was helping out my professor, Dr. Austin Allen, on a project in partnership with Maurice Cox at Small Center. The project was in collaboration with the New Orleans Mardi Gras Indians. Through interviews, research, and visualization, our work would perhaps inspire design concepts for a future campus development. As part of this project, my role was to document the New Orleans Mardi Gras Indian tribes.

My real experience in public interest design began on Mardi Gras day in New Orleans, 2013, with a camera in my hand. This was one of my first assignments, filming the New Orleans Mardi Gras Indians' Big Chief Howard Miller of the Creole Wild West. The occasion was special because I was getting access to Chief Howard on Mardi Gras day, when he and his tribe would be masking through the city, looking for other

tribes and showcasing traditions that are on display once a year, and only in New Orleans! I arrived bright and early, with my camera and a backpack full of rented equipment, sitting on the Creole Wild West porch. I had imagined a knock on the door would be all I would need to get in the house, but I was mistaken. It was Mardi Gras day, and these men were putting the final touches on suits they'd sown for an entire year, dressing and embodying the spirit and persona of the Mardi Gras Indians that would carry them through the streets of New Orleans. To further complicate things, it was raining. The suits are made of beads and feathers, which don't mix so well with heavy rain. They were not coming out. And they were not letting me and my camera in that day. A Spy Boy opened the door, but only to inform me that I would not be let inside. After about an hour of sitting in the rain with camera equipment, I got the hint.

But I kept bringing my camera to New Orleans. And eventually interviews were scheduled. Bertrand Butler, the New Orleans Mardi Gras Indian Council's director, arranged the interviews and got us access. That semester our student crews filmed over a dozen New Orleans Mardi Gras Indian Chiefs, mostly in their living rooms. I edited the footage and showed it to an auditorium full of design students working on project proposals for this same community. The students learned, and I gained a sense of place and self, through telling the story of the New Orleans Mardi Gras Indians with my camera. Small Center, then called the Tulane City Center, facilitated a planning effort on behalf of the New Orleans Mardi Gras Indian Council to envision a cultural campus. In support of this effort, I contributed many hours of footage from interviewing Chiefs and documenting Mardi Gras Indians. The digital archive I created offered research to inform the design and still serves as archival material for the Council to preserve and share their culture for future generations. The planning study led to a grant, and the grant led to a new role for me: project manager for the New Orleans Mardi Gras Indians Cultural Campus.

// ABOVE: LaSalle St. composite by Matt Williams

// PREVIOUS: Chief Howard Miller masks on Mardi Gras Day, Photo: Matt Williams

Some of the caretakers of place and culture I know and have studied are closely guarded people who will reveal an entirely different world to you once they trust you. Starting as a cameraman was my way into their world. It was a difficult way to build rapport, albeit it was eventually earned. But I really earned the trust of the New Orleans Mardi Gras Indians over coffee. Coffee with Bertrand Butler helped transform my understanding of what Public Interest Design is all about and how I would need to master it as a skill to be effective within the fields of planning and design. I cannot recall who asked who for that first cup of coffee. But, eventually, it was a routine: Uncle Bert and I got a cup of coffee every day at a small coffee shop off St. Charles Ave. We'd sit for an hour, sometimes longer, and he would tell me the history or the Mardi Gras Indian Culture, details about how different tribes came to be, about legendary Chiefs, and other real New Orleans history. It was all the information I simply could not have known to ask during those early camera interviews. Through these daily conversations, we truly got to know each other as individuals beyond our immediate interests. I came to call him "Uncle Bert," and I still expect to hear "What's up, Neph?" whenever we speak. Our coffee routine humanized us to each other and gave us the focused dialogue we needed to develop real trust. Each day we returned with a genuine desire to keep learning with, and from, each other. That was 2014-2015. The New Orleans Mardi Gras Indian Cultural Campus officially opened in 2019.

I'm grateful for the opportunity to have honed my skills working with Austin Allen, Maurice Cox, and the New Orleans Mardi Gras Indians. Those skills still serve me. I've been blessed to participate in national, award-winning projects, lead organizations, speak at national conferences, and take on meaningful roles in the City of Detroit. "Public Interest" is embedded in a lot of the work I do now. As often as I can, I try to begin talking to people in the neighborhood, at a local spot, preferably with a good cup of coffee and a good story to hear. This is where real "engagement" happens.

SECTION TWO

Studying Design Alongside Communities

3

Making, Doing, Testing

"As a body of work...the projects are a collection of prototypes for a city created through collective processes of discussion and action."

To date, Small Center has constructed forty-seven structures through its design-build studios. Nationally, this work is recognized for choreographing care in engagement alongside care in craft. Locally, its design-build projects have established a reputation for participatory work that leads to tangible outcomes. Tangible outcomes are valuable in a city that has undergone numerous public planning workshops to inform policy and development. Residents and nonprofit organizations in New Orleans are particularly sensitive to planning fatigue. Small Center's work offers a counterpoint. While often modest in scale, the built structures it creates represent a physical outcome shaped by community voice and tailored to an organization's needs. For many partners, the resulting structure serves as a symbol of the importance of their organizational goals, holding space as a physical declaration of the value of their mission. As a body of work across the city, Small Center projects are a collection of prototypes for a city created through collective processes of discussion and action.

Small Center's work is community-led and grounded in real needs, as defined by the communities most impacted. Its form is shaped by another constituency: architecture students. As a university-based community design center, Small Center bears a responsibility to educate and mentor the next generation of designers. This educational mission is made possible by the Center's position within the Tulane School of Architecture, which provides some financial support to the Center, as well

// A student walks a group of middle school students through a 3-d model of Sugar Roots Farm.

// Custom booths with sliding privacy panels separate work spaces at STEM Library Lab.

as access to university expertise and infrastructure. As the School's outreach arm, Small Center offers two to three courses per year and a variety of paid internships and research appointments for advanced architecture students to contribute to the work while earning course credit or wages. Center staff take this charge seriously, and each project's planning includes careful scrutiny of the specific learning opportunities offered to future design professionals. Project managers consider what skills students can be expected to bring to a project as paid interns and what skills can be realistically taught if the project is included in a semester-long course. Opportunities also exist for faculty whose research overlaps with the needs of the nonprofit project partners.

In the years following Hurricane Katrina, Tulane University used its status as an anchor institution in the city to contribute to rebuilding efforts. The University centered its efforts on addressing community-defined needs. Mobilizing its students to participate, Tulane emphasized civic engagement and supported opportunities for coursework that included public service, or service-learning. New branches of the university emerged to guide this work, including the Center for Engaged Learning and Teaching and the Center for Public Service. Tulane emerged as a leader in promoting civic engagement within higher education at a time when engaged learning was gaining traction nationally. Small Center benefited from the opportunity to work with like-minded academic partners, and the institutional support it received from a university uniquely receptive to community-based work and civic engagement in the classroom was invaluable.

As has been described in previous chapters, design engagement takes time and has the potential to extend or disrupt typical project schedules. Rigid expectations for the outcomes of advanced studio courses and inflexible, semester-based schedules create pressure to adhere to a tight timeline of research, design ideation, and construction, all punctuated by engagement activities and skill-building workshops. Small Center uses a team-based approach to balance these often conflicting needs. For each project, a studio instructor leads design development and supports student educational goals, while a dedicated project manager serves as a thought partner and coordinator for engagement activities, material purchases, and other administrative tasks. Three-to-six months of preparation go into setting up the relationships that will sustain engagement. During this time, multiple meetings with the project partner determine a scope that serves its goals and is achievable within a short, sixteen-week semester. Student interns are involved in these conversations, shaping the project and building trust with community partners.

Students also help to assess each project's outcomes. After construction, Small Center follows up to observe how things are used, how materials are holding up, and how it might address any problems. Summer Public Interest Design Fellows participate in these site visits to previous projects, learning from past work. These post-construction evaluations inform future projects and foster ongoing relationships with past partners.

Small-scale design-build projects are at the heart of Small Center's work. Students see a project from concept through construction, realizing projects in one-semester studio courses. Design-build is an opportunity to gain experience with material exploration, model building, full-scale mockup testing, and on-site construction as creative and analytical processes. Students' built mock-ups and models aid in design conversations with community members, and they understand the value of these tools in communicating their ideas in practice. Students also learn the embodied knowledge of construction skills: the variety of joining methods, the appropriate order of assembling different materials, or the need to account for space for fingers and tools. The Center's expectation is not for students to become skilled carpenters, though care in craft is important. Students leave the course with an understanding of the variety of questions that inform efficient and innovative design. They learn to form these questions at the scale of construction details, and they learn to communicate their solutions through physical artifacts that can be discussed with collaborators. Developing a design from conception to completion helps students understand

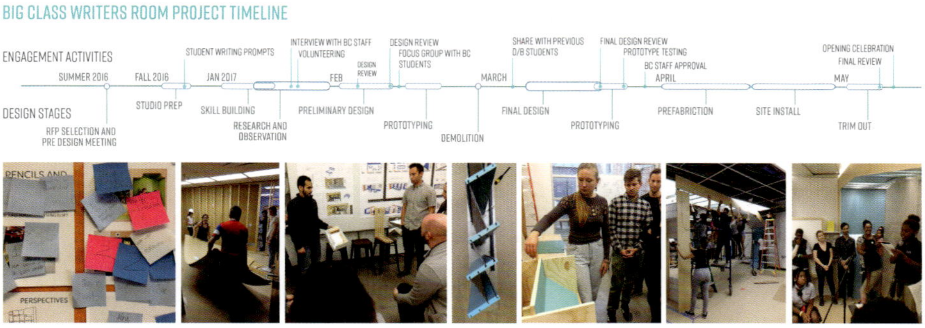

// Balancing engagement, design, skill building, and fabrication in 15 weeks.

how the design phase extends into the building process, including adjustments and real-time problem-solving. Students come to appreciate the difficulty of achieving a carefully crafted structure and the need for precise detailing to attain that goal.

Design studios include assigned research into the cultural and historical contexts of any given project, site, and partner, including the issues on which it focuses, from urban agriculture, to live music, to STEM education. This research aims to keep students mindful of, and responsive to, the place in which they are working; Tulane architecture students hone their design and construction skills in the city environment and must respond to these inputs as appropriate. New Orleanians claim space through ephemeral parades and unique and colorful local architecture. Residents express identity through craft and ritual.

Indeed, cultural traditions are often forms of craft: the elaborate beadwork and sewing of Mardi Gras Indian suits, the careful creation of a flavorful meal, or the posting of ad hoc and artful street signs across town. New Orleans is a community of makers from which students have much to learn. Within the city, Small Center's design-build projects are a tangible demonstration of community needs being taken seriously and community ideas being realized. As physical transformations of the urban environment, Small Center's built work demonstrates many possibilities for the city's future. In some cases, the structures serve as prototypes of new forms that bridge historic New Orleans building typologies with contemporary concerns and materials. In other instances, built projects represent proof that community-led initiatives have a protected place and value in New Orleans. As a model for future design leaders and advocates, the Center's approach illustrates how all residents benefit when design is not treated as a luxury–accessible only to those with power or money–but as a tool for prototyping a city shaped by the ideas and needs of its inhabitants.

BUILD

Grow Dat Youth Farm

Cultivating Leadership on an Urban Agriculture Campus, 2009-2011

Grow Dat Youth Farm was founded by Johanna Gilligan and informed by her experience working in environmental education and student-led school food reform. The program aimed to address the need for youth employment and leadership opportunities while providing access to fresh food. The youth of New Orleans lack job opportunities and thus the possibility to gain income and skills that come with first-time jobs. The few jobs available to New Orleans high school aged students are in the fast-food service industry which compounds nutritional issues, and working according to inconvenient shift times often compromise students' academic growth. Small Center was the incubator and fiscal home for the program vision, in addition to designing and constructing its campus in New Orleans City Park.

Through multiple, semester-long studios, held across two years, Small Center designed and constructed the 6,000-square-foot facility and four-acre farm site.[29] The design engaged the specific environmental challenges of converting a former golf course into agricultural production with a sensitivity to modeling sustainable

// ABOVE: Students enjoy the outdoor classroom and training kitchen. Photo: Will Crocker
// OPPOSITE: Grow Dat student employees learn about sustainable food production.

practices. The learning facilities and growing spaces were located to preserve existing trees and to manage stormwater on-site as a means of protecting the health of a nearby bayou waterway. Shaded rest and cooling spaces are woven throughout the site, from preserved groves of trees to new plantings. Water is managed and filtered on-site through planted swales. Crop irrigation and water sequestration are integrated with the building design, and wastewater is treated on-site. As a former golf course, the soil quality has taken years to rebuild through sustainable agricultural practices.

All structures were located to create an entry court to the farm and to make use of land unsuitable for crop production. The design is constructed from seven recycled shipping containers and recycled steel trusses to form a large, covered outdoor classroom, offices, food processing spaces, and a storage facility. The containers are positioned to form a buffer from the nearby highway and to shelter the program spaces from sun exposure. These material choices support the preservation of trees. The shipping containers require only point-loaded foundations at their corners, making long, efficient spans and sparing the adjacent cypress tree roots from disruptive excavation.[30] Each shipping container is shaded with vine-covered façade screens and rain screen protection. Subcontractors were hired for crane operation and electrical work, but all other work was completed by Tulane architecture students, from foundation to finished space.

The architecture allows flexibility for a variety of youth activities and prioritizes environmentally responsible stewardship of a public site. Growing food on-site serves multiple purposes in support of youth leadership. The produce is a marketable commodity and youth workers gain experience in marketing and sales. Classes use seasonal produce to teach healthy food preparation, healthy living, and eating choices. Participants take a portion of the produce home to share with family and friends. Classes teach students about agriculture as well as leadership and social responsibility. Youth workers, volunteers, and staff learn alongside one another in lessons that foreground critical histories of land and labor. Now seven acres, the program continues to evolve. In response, Grow Dat is currently developing plans for an interpretive pathway that will take visitors throughout both swampy and agricultural areas to experience the history of the land by engaging with it directly.

Grow Dat remains the largest project built by Small Center. It helped set a standard for excellence in design in the Center's built projects and provided high visibility for both Grow Dat and Small Center, garnering attention and awards. Unique funding opportunities and a somewhat flexible curricular schedule allowed the project to be completed over the course of two years, but lessons learned at Grow Dat also helped to solidify Small Center's shorter, one-semester project time frame for subsequent projects.

Throughout the design process, Small Center connected Grow Dat Youth Farm to other organizations and community leaders working to improve the lives of young

// The primary structure contains a variety of gathering spaces. Photo: Will Crocker

// ABOVE: Grow Dat's entry ramp, crossing over green infrastructure aimed at flood mitigation. Photo: Will Crocker

people in New Orleans. In the years since, Grow Dat's leadership has continued to steward a community that cares deeply about the project. Recently, this community of supporters came together to ensure Grow Dat's future. In Spring 2024, City Park released a master plan for park improvements that included a new road through the Grow Dat site. The master plan illustrated City Park's intention to evict the farm when its lease expired in 2027. However, community members rallied around the farm. The farm hosted public meetings to imagine a more community-driven masterplan, with young people as facilitators and speakers. After months of meetings, petitions, and media coverage, the City Park leadership changed course and renewed Grow Dat's lease. The farm's future in City Park was secured through the model of collaborative leadership that Grow Dat teaches.

[29] Emilie Taylor Welty and Scott Bernhard, "Grow Dat Youth Farm," *The Design-Build Studio: Crafting Meaningful Work in Architecture Education*, ed. Tolya Stonorov (Routledge, 2017), 189-198.

[30] Scott Bernhard, "Notes on the Intersection of Architecture and Social Entrepreneurship," *Working Out: Thinking While Building: Proceedings of the 33rd ACSA Fall Conference*, ed. Ted Cavanaugh, Ursula Hartig, and Sergio Palleroni (ACSA Press, 2014), 263-272.

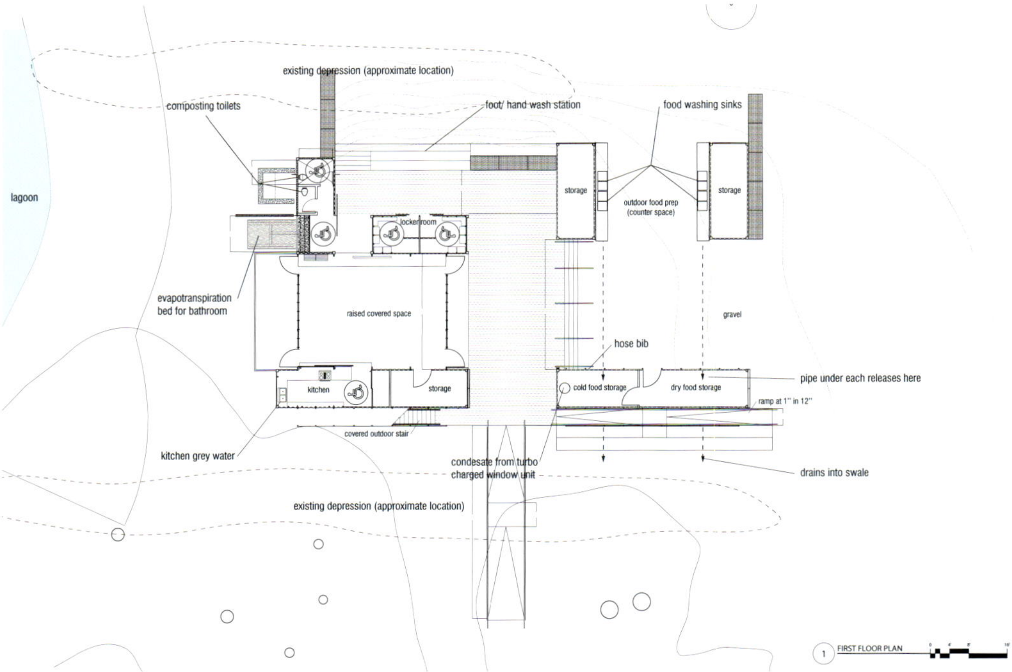

"I learned how to test the soil and to work it sustainably. And I was bringing home kale and chard, which we couldn't afford to buy." -Grow Dat student employee

BUILD

Community Book Center

A New Interior for a Neighborhood Gathering Place, 2016

Vera Warren-Williams started selling books in 1983. At the time, she was a substitute teacher and wanted to address the lack of books by, and about, Black people in her students' courses. She began bringing children's books by Black authors to school and quickly began filling requests outside of the classroom. Her passion for books evolved into a business. She began selling books out of the back of her car, and then from a friend's home-based business before taking on a brick-and-mortar location. In 2003, Community Book Center (CBC) moved to Bayou Road, where it has become a neighborhood cornerstone. The CBC acts as a local hangout in a historic and rapidly changing neighborhood. In this capacity, the store and Ms. Vera have partnered with Small Center in a range of capacities. The design-build studio which supported a refresh of the store's interior served as a signal of a commitment to protecting and investing in sites significant to the local community.

// ABOVE: Rendering imagines a dynamic new children's reading area.
// OPPOSITE: Proprietor Vera Warren-Williams reads to children in the completed space.
Photo: Michael Wong

Small Center first worked with Ms. Vera as an active participant in two previous projects along Bayou Road. The first project, with Broad Community Connections, translated the City of New Orleans's plans for streetscape improvements into easily understandable drawings in order to take suggestions from merchants; the project also created a graphic, foldable pocket guide to help promote Bayou Road businesses. Community Book Center was also a participant in the Façade RENEW program, described in Chapter 2. Over time, these small interventions combined to strengthen neighborhood anchors and support Bayou Road's community of Black women-owned businesses.

Bayou Road is the oldest road in New Orleans. The six-block stretch from Esplanade to Broad Street is a center for independent retail shops. Community Book Center is seen as a flagship of retail on the street. It is a hangout for multiple generations: a space to do homework, a place to gossip, and a spot to meet up with friends. The store hosts art shows, storytelling events, book discussions, and markets. The store was furnished through the creative use of hand-me-downs. Video store racks were used to display art and books. A mix of upholstered and folding chairs were repurposed for hosted gatherings. Ms. Vera and the store manager, Mama Jennifer, worked with what they had, but the ad hoc setup presented challenges. The racks damaged merchandise. The nondescript interior didn't signal the care and intention of the store's owner. The store faced other challenges. In 2016, independent bookstores across the country suffered from the convenience of online sales, and the pressure of gentrification was felt along Bayou Road. Small Center's Spring 2016 design-build studio offered an opportunity to refresh the interior and signal the store's identity as a Black educational space.

Tulane students began familiarizing themselves with Community Book Center's mission by reading. Each student selected a book from the store to analyze. The experience of reading books that represent the lives of Black characters illustrated the nuance involved in representing cultural identity with care and authenticity. The reading assignment laid the groundwork for conversations with Ms. Vera and her clientele about representation. The assignment also challenged students to hone their skills in fabrication and conceptual design. Each student designed and built a furniture piece that could hold a person reading a book and also display a book. Reading discussions and material investigations informed the development of joinery methods inspired by African textiles. Kente, a traditional cloth stemming from Asante culture, is a form of expressing history and values through the weaving of different patterns. These expressive patterns were mimicked through the joining of plywood end grain to echo the cloth and illustrations of contemporary Afro-centric literature, both of which are sold in the bookstore.

By spending time in the Community Book Center, students developed an understanding of the store's day-to-day use and the circulation patterns of the neighborhood. This

knowledge expanded through a survey of the bookstore's customers and staff. Field trips to other Black spaces in New Orleans allowed students to gain perspective on the space as a cultural hub. A series of focus groups gave feedback on design drawings and initial analyses of the store's needs, and prototypes supported further refinement. Focus group conversations included other leaders of neighborhood cultural institutions, who helped to identify the opportunities for Community Book Center to strengthen its place within the communities it serves and to expand its market to new customers.

// ABOVE: Students develop wood details for Center tables.
// OPPOSITE: Mobile bookshelves can be moved to accommodate community events. Photo: Michael Wong

The final design for the bookstore served a multi-generational community. The front of the store centered the needs of children and community gathering, with dedicated stadium seating for larger gatherings and kids' height tables and seating. The checkout remained in the same area it had occupied previously; however, it was reoriented to serve in two directions, the kids' area, whose counter was shorter, and the adult bookstore area with added retail. The checkout and the pivot wall act as a threshold between the conversational public space and the quiet, intimate space of the bookstacks in the back half of the store. The pivot wall acts as storage and blocks off the back of the store for public events. Bookshelves line the back half of the walls while rolling shelves in the interior allow for flexibility in the center space.

Since its opening, Community Books has leveraged its new space to hold book signings and pop-up jewelry and art events. Additionally, Tulane students updated the branding identity for the store, creating a new logo with a color scheme that matches an exterior mural by a local artist, Brandan "Bmike" Odums.

BUILD

Ozanam Inn Day Space

Outdoor, Protected Space for the Unhoused Population, 2016 (demolished 2021)

Ozanam Inn is one of a variety of organizations committed to addressing the chronic and complicated issue of homelessness in New Orleans. As a special work of St. Vincent de Paul, Ozanam Inn has provided aid, food, clothing, and shelter for over sixty years. Staff and volunteers work with each client's individual needs by offering case management and counseling, job and life skills training, treatment for physical, dental and mental health concerns, legal counsel, and a mailing address. Uncommon among local shelters, Ozanam provides space for their clients not just at night, but throughout the day. This covered outdoor space accommodates seating and offers some protection from the weather and is in constant use. Through time on-site and focus groups with clients and staff, the design team learned the multiple functions that this narrow, ad hoc space serves. The seating area facilitated line-up for meals at Ozanam, storage of clients' belongings, hosting of social functions, and use as a

// ABOVE: Small Center students engage with Ozanam Inn leadership, staff, and clientele.
// OPPOSITE: Clients enjoy the new covered seating area. Photo: Neil Alexander Photography

waiting area for access to the Inn's many services. The existing condition consisted of simple wood benches, utilitarian fencing, and trash bins. During rainstorms, areas of the space had previously flooded and damaged client's belongings.

The design needed to accommodate these many uses, solve the complex environmental issues of the site, and be constructed without interrupting ongoing services. The design team's work centered on the question: How can architecture affirm human dignity? The design process engaged clients through conversations centered on drawings and prototypes and drew inspiration from the ideas generated through these engagements. The resulting design addressed the immediate problems of the space. The site strategy addressed concerns heard during focus groups, such as the clients' desire to see their bicycles and belongings while sitting on the deck. Material details signaled the care for clients and staff. Motivational phrases were painted into the translucent ceiling and different groupings of seats allowed clients to choose to sit alone or in sociable pairs.

The outdoor day space featured a long, undulating roofline. The roof was lifted significantly higher than the flat roof it replaced, capturing additional light and air while projecting further from the building to ensure continued protection from weather. A raised deck and benches with built-in storage ensured that clients' belongings remained dry, avoiding localized flooding common to the parking lot. The benches served as dividers for mealtime line up, without creating a sense of enclosure in the area. The space recalled the feeling of sitting on a New Orleans porch, with a traditional sky-blue ceiling. A service area contained, and screened, trash collection and allowed visual access to dedicated and secure bike parking. A new ramp and stair integrated the day space with Ozanam's primary client entrance, simplifying ADA access to the building and services. The completed project improved the outdoor space available to Ozanam's clients, providing a comfortable, social, and inspirational area with better access to the many services available on-site.

In 2021, Ozanam Inn relocated to nearby Poydras Street after the unexpected sale of its building by the owner. Through a major fundraising campaign, Ozanam was able to complete the purchase and renovation of a new structure that allowed for the first-time provision of shelter for female clients, along with dedicated dental and healthcare screening rooms. Though in a new location with different site conditions, Ozanam adapted Small Center's approach to sheltered outdoor space, creating a shaded and weather protected area for clients lining up for meals and overnight lodging.

// OPPOSITE: New decking and seating created comfortable places for socializing, meal-line up, and more. Photo: Neil Alexander Photography
// BELOW: Students install modular triangular roof pieces that were built off-site

BUILD

Hotel Hope Hexspace

A New Playspace for Mothers and Children, 2019

Hotel Hope is an interfaith, nonprofit organization that provides housing and services to women and children living through homelessness. The emergency housing program at Hotel Hope recognizes that housing crises can occur at all hours and offers support on a twenty-four-hour basis. The organization responded to the annual Request for Projects with a proposal to transform a courtyard parking lot at their emergency shelter into a playscape. The project recognizes the need for children of all ages to have safe spaces to play, bike, and hang out. The design process embraced the importance of playfulness as an essential part of creating and testing design forms.

The project began with an analysis of the existing courtyard and its use as a parking lot. Art activities and conversations with children and mothers staying at Hotel

Hope guided the development of the project's goals. Children and mothers imagined a lush oasis with spaces where they could connect through play. Early design ideas explored sandboxes, canopies, tunnels, and play structures. Discussions with staff, board members, residents, and design critics refined the proposals to prioritize durable, warm materials and to create a space that supports children of various ages. The space also needed to accommodate meals, outdoor celebrations, and informal gathering.

The resulting scheme, "Hexscape," includes a tunnel, a shaky bridge, and a music wall that offer space for climbing and sensory play. An alligator mulch pit is a refuge of younger kids. Planting and a custom mural enhance the feeling of an outdoor room dedicated to joyful play. Design for each component was developed through the construction, and testing of, a series of prototypes. Full-scale mockups of the tunnel allowed students to identify an appropriate size for children. Additional mockups helped to refine the construction method for the tunnel and to locate peepholes within the form. Material investigations led to custom bricks, dyed and formed for the seat walls that edge each planter. Prototypes and material tests are important tools for developing designs and can be particularly useful for getting feedback from the intended users of the space. With a real budget and timeline, students learned to

// ABOVE: Renderings picture possible playscape options to be shared with residents.

// OPPOSITE: Resident children show Tulane students how they use the space for play.

balance the role of these tests for design development with the cost in terms of time and materials.

Students honed their understanding of the construction process through building and unbuilding. The site design required the demolition of specific areas of existing concrete. The formwork for the tunnel was constructed at the Small Center's shop, moved to the Hotel Hope site, and concrete was poured in place. Soil was moved into place and compacted to form hills, and site walls were constructed to form seating and frame each playspace. Like many projects, the site design and construction has continued to evolve. Hotel Hope led painting projects on the alligator and tunnel, and Small Center replaced the hill's grass with turf upon observing the extreme wear-and-tear of many children climbing and jumping from it on a daily basis. These post-construction changes ensure that the project continues to be an asset for Hotel Hope and the families who call it home.

// LEFT: Students prototype and build formwork.
// OPPOSITE: Completed playscape elements include a curved tunnel with dappled sunlight.

Smile!
Dream Big!

"It is a rich experience full of learning and hands-on work that will make you a sensible, better designer and human being. [It] pushed me to refine and deepen my conception of how architecture can be utilized as a tool for social justice." -Small Center student

LSU

VISION/BUILD

Materials of Abolition

Seeding Change at the Abolitionist's Sanctuary & John Thompson Legacy Center, 2023-2024

Small Center's work is informed by the acknowledgement that architecture and the design professions are entangled with systems of harm and destruction. The Materials of Abolition studio emerged from a collaboration with local organizations working to challenge systems of harm through the creation of systems of care, healing, and reparations. As a design studio, this partnership explored alternative material choices to define an architecture guided by interconnection and the reduction of future harms.

The studio was informed by partnerships with organizations working on prison abolition through creative practice. John Thompson spent eighteen years in prison for a crime he did not commit, including fourteen years on death row. Upon his

release, he dedicated his life to criminal justice reform and founded Resurrection After Exoneration (RAE), now the John Thompson Legacy Center (JTLC). The organization serves formerly incarcerated individuals and other people impacted by the criminal legal system. JTLC partners with the Abolitionist's Apothecary and Sanctuary, two co-located projects that grow healing herbal medicine and offer workshops that explore what plants can teach us about abolition. Solitary Gardens is a project led by artist jackie summell that evokes the possibility of a landscape without prisons through a process of collaborative garden-making. Each of these organizations partnered with Small Center on past initiatives, some of which are described in Chapter 6. In this studio, Small Center's approach was informed and shaped by the material ethics of summell's work to help develop a vision for the JTLC's future.

Students began by exploring the material processes present at Solitary Gardens' Andry Street location in the Lower Ninth Ward. At the garden, crops associated with chattel slavery are grown, including cotton, indigo, tobacco, and sugarcane. Working together, students experienced the physical labor required to tend, harvest, and process these plant materials into usable products. Experiments and further research supported the development of new materials aimed to reduce carbon emissions and model sustainability in social, economic, and environmental relationships. Innovation, teamwork, and failure underpinned the work. The process of experimentation offered a new perspective on the questions within all design-build studios. How can locally-sourced materials impact a design's carbon footprint? What are the opportunities for using bio-based materials in architecture? How do we design with a respect for the skill and embodied knowledge of construction tradespeople? What aspects of this site and this client will inform a specific approach to the craft and history of construction?

A series of material tests informed final installations at the JTLC's Abolitionist Sanctuary. Collectively, the studio demonstrated the potential of cob and local clay,

// ABOVE: Students constructed an archway to test sustainable materials.

// OPPOSITE: Mycelium roof tiles feature on a local community garden pavilion.

wattle and daub, oyster shell aggregates, bagasse bricks, and mycelium shingles, as locally sourced construction materials. Alongside the physical demonstrations, students created maps and diagrams illustrating their research on the environmental, social and economic sustainability of various construction approaches. The anti-capitalist, abolitionist, and collective ethics of the project's partners offered an emphasis on the full life cycle implications of material choices: each material's origins, its processing by human labor, its assembly, and its decay. The studio explored the multiple environmental and social consequences of the architecture and construction industries. Students gained skills for foregrounding the invisible labor and potential harms associated with their design decisions.

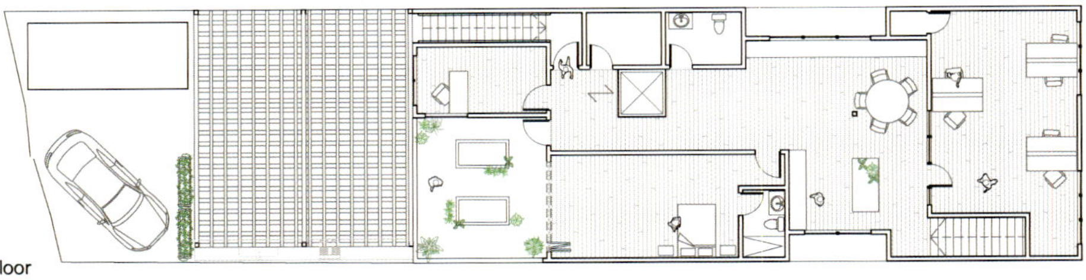

Second Floor

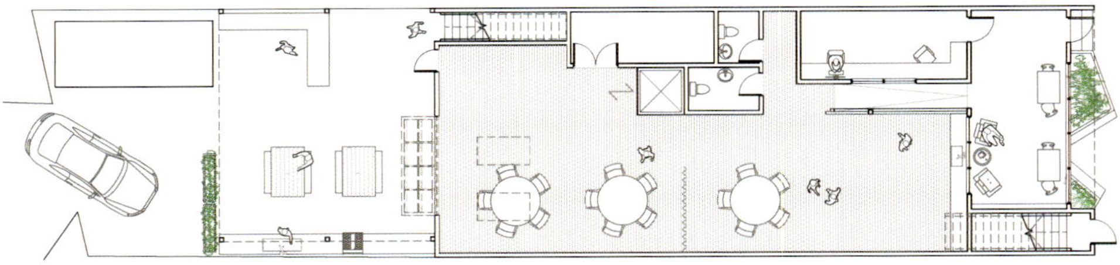

First Floor

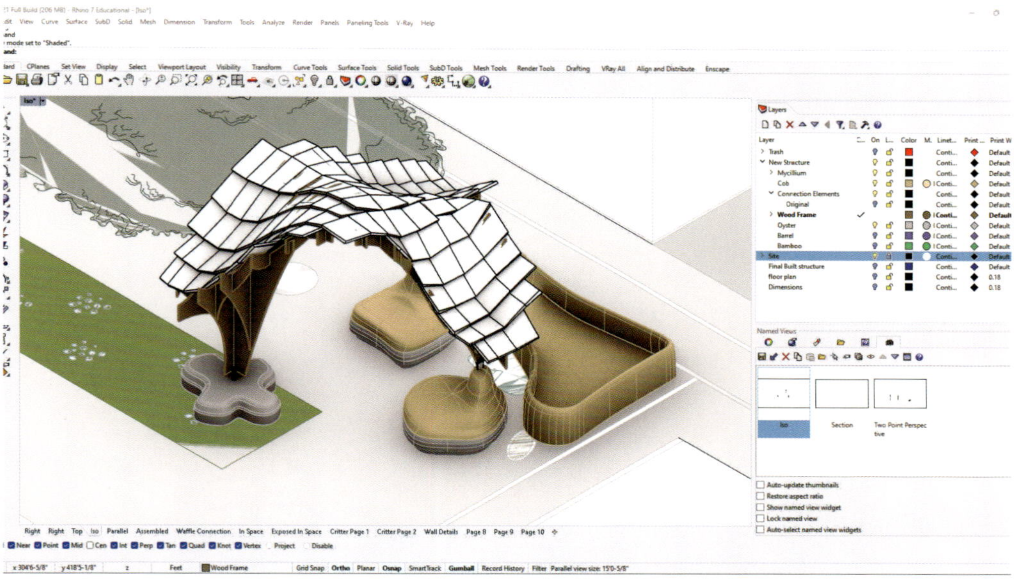

// ABOVE: 3D modeling allowed for the creation of complex pavilion shapes.
// ABOVE + OPPOSITE: Visioning concepts for the John Thompson Legacy Center's renovation and expansion.

An Architecture of Compassion

Doug Harmon

The former Small Center design-build leader talks about using new methods and materials to bring dignity to everyday spaces.

If I have a hero in architecture, it is Samuel "Sambo" Mockbee. As a young, idealistic person from Mississippi studying architecture, I was fortunate to cross paths with Sambo and began following his career as he created and led Auburn's Rural Studio. There was a refreshing spirit of humility that seemed to permeate his words, his teaching, and the resulting student work. And yet this humble spirit was also coupled with a deep conviction and wild-eyed boldness in the power of design to move, heal, inspire, and transform people and communities–what could be termed "an architecture of compassion." This conviction led him, and his students, to the heart of underserved communities with the belief that good design, capital "D" Design, is not a luxury reserved for the affluent but rather reaches its highest calling in places that are regularly overlooked, neglected, and marginalized. (The word

"underserved" plays tricks with my brain – it wants to instead read "undeserving," which couldn't be further from the heart of the matter. Thankfully, Sambo and the Rural Studio helped to forge the path in the opposite direction.) Through Sambo's influence, my convictions for design were given shape, depth, and color.

In my work with Small Center, I was fortunate to collaborate with students who shared, challenged, and further shaped my convictions about the power of design while working on multiple community-engaged design projects. It was at Small Center that students and I were given the opportunity to work alongside community partners with a deep, proven commitment to serving vulnerable communities in our city. With each project, we had to wrestle with translating our "high-minded" design convictions into a street-level material reality that advanced the mission of our partners to the real benefit of the people with whom they (and now we) worked and served. And with each project, it was the students and I who were impacted most by the grace, wisdom, and care we were shown from the organizations and people with whom we worked through the entire process, from design to construction. The broader hope for the students is that these experiences convince them that they have unique and vitally needed gifts to contribute to the work of hope and healing in overlooked places.

We were asked to design and construct a new sheltered outdoor day space for the largely unhoused clients of Ozanam Inn. The north star for the project was Ozanam Inn's stated mission:

> At Ozanam Inn, our immediate priority is to offer aid and comfort to the poor and needy in our community by providing basic human needs, such as: food, shelter, and clothing. While the foundation of our organization's mission, it is only part of the work we do at Ozanam Inn. To end their suffering, we work with all individuals who come to us for assistance to move them from homelessness and hopelessness to independent living and a renewed feeling of HOPE.

As a design-build team, through regular conversations with the leadership and staff at Ozanam, as well as the unhoused clients they serve, our task was to understand at the most basic human level what the layered needs were and how thoughtful design and construction could anticipate, meet, and alleviate those needs to the best of our ability. These needs had to become design decisions and material results. Through those on-site conversations, we deepened our connections to the common denominators of our shared humanity. We began to understand a little better, if even slightly, the daily burdens of the unhoused women and men and the need for

// OPPOSITE: Ozanam clients chose messages to be stenciled on the underside of the roof. Photo: Neil Alexander Photography

the day space to be a place of refuge, of rest, of community, and, in the process, to offer "a renewed feeling of HOPE." By "burdens," I don't only mean each person's weighted multitude of worries and concerns; I also mean the physical burden of maintaining, moving, and securing their possessions in bags and cases wherever they go and the physical toll that takes on a body.

Ozanam Inn is an amazing place of comprehensive care. In addition to providing overnight shelter to hundreds of men, they also provide critical support services and three meals a day to the broader community in need. In order to provide over 300 meals at a time, they need the process of waiting for, and proceeding to, meals to be as clearly organized and orderly as possible. When we arrived onsite, shelter from the sun and rain was provided by a low, horizontal aluminum roof with a strong institutional quality, and a six-foot chain link fence was used to help form the space for lining up for meals. I don't fault Ozanam Inn for these choices–they were simply solving a need in the most basic manner. However, the space suffered greatly from the lack of imaginative power, the power of good, human-directed design.

An arresting revelation came to me during this process and I have carried it with me to all of my work to this day, which is we are not being called to give dignity to anyone. Each person already possesses dignity, however much of their daily existence might ignore or deny that dignity. Our responsibility, by contrast, was to think about the ways in which our designs at multiple scales affirmed and reinforced this dignity (and ours as well). Can innate dignity really be addressed through design and materially constructed spaces and objects?

Drawing from the conversations we had with many of the users of the space, we began to develop what I call the "spiritual program" for the project–the DNA that would work its way through the project and guide our decisions, and that would hopefully lead to something that was much more than the sum of its particular design decisions, allowing the day space to be "symphonic." The students and I developed a litany of words to try to help give greater collective understanding and agreement to what we were working towards. A word like "hope" does not have a particular physical connotation per se. But "lift" does. As do "levity," "lightness," and "openness." How do these words direct decisions about forms, materials, assemblies, and details? How do they help us think about color, where to use it, and what types?

We also thought about how to be intentional in affirming the dignity of anyone using the space. We directed our designs to think about reinforcing one's humanity, his physical being, through the scale of the space(s), the materials a person will touch when he sits, the angles of the benches providing comfort and rest, what he sees over time, in different seasons, and how he can choose to sit alone or with others.

One of the most surprisingly radical moments in the project's construction occurred in demolition. It was the moment we cut down the chain link fence. It seemed to usher in new life, as if the place could now breathe freely for the first time. From there, the project worked to expand and celebrate this new capacity for breathing.

The next "radical" move in the project was creating a wooden deck to lift the "floor" of the day space, which was previously the same asphalt ground of the adjacent

// BELOW: The completed "day space" roof and seating area. Photo: Neil Alexander Photography

parking lot, by a mere four inches. What seemed like such a small gesture had a profound impact on the overall quality and perception of the space. Women and men were lifted up, removing their feet and their possessions from the wet ground when it rained. The space for them was set apart, no longer by the margins of the parking lot, but, through the use of the wood, to a warm and resonant space that was now intentionally defined. Likewise, the volume of this space was greatly enhanced and increased through a new, triangulated roof. The form of the roof was intended to break up the overall scale of the long, linear space, while creating a new sense of scale under each "bay" that would be conducive to a greater intimation of gathering and belonging. We thought about how the structure participates in this quality of lifting and lightness, separating materials into their individual performances, putting space between layers, and articulating the light connections in their joints and details. The roof trusses became open, dynamic, and colorful, animating the light through the new translucent roof. At the suggestion of some of the unhoused clients, we sought ways to introduce encouraging text and more color in subtle and somewhat surprising ways with the hope that their discovery in time would bring delight.

Finally, we designed and built benches–of steel for a sense of surety and wood for warmth of touch--anchored to the wood deck to provide ample storage and comfort for a day's rest. The scale of the benches was varied, accommodating two or three people with small side tables built in-between for individual use, or for use as a space to speak and connect across. In place of the fence, the benches organized the lines forming before meals. This function only becomes apparent when needed and recedes into a place of respite soon after. I have come to think about sitting on the benches as an act of unweighting.

What we were after, ultimately, was a built work that embodied hope and materially communicated care in such a way as to add dimension and reach to the great work of Ozanam Inn. This required a commitment on our part to show up and be present, to engage the community where they were, to work through our deep-seated limits and biases, to hear their stories and to learn of their deepest needs and hopes, to be better listeners than speakers, and to recognize our shared humanity. It also required a commitment to putting our whole selves into the work, to the rigor of iterating ideas in collaboration and materially testing them through prototyping, and to recognize when something was good or just wasn't good enough. And it required us to be welcomed, humbled, helped, and changed in this community through the process. The great hope is that someone sat differently in that space and felt a little lighter.

Growing Together

Johanna Gilligan

The founding director of Grow Dat Youth Farm describes how Small Center's partnership helped to realize the Farm as a place and a program.

Grow Dat Youth Farm is a place made for young adults. The farm is a seven-acre site located in the heart of City Park, a 1300-acre oasis of live oak trees, Works Progress Administration bayous, curated and wild spaces—all near and dear to New Orleanians. Grow Dat came to life in the post-Katrina remaking of the city, at a time when residents and civic leaders were in the throes of rebuilding so much from scratch—a moment of extreme creativity born out of necessity.

Grow Dat is a place where young people from across the city come to grow food, build leadership skills, learn about the history and ecology of the land, and explore the food system as it relates to systemic inequities in America. This combination gives participants space to develop into young leaders with a vision for a more just and sustainable food system and world.

The farm's location in City Park is no coincidence. When launching the organization, we spent time considering in which public spaces young people from across the city would feel at home. Like so many American cities, New Orleans is shaped by a history of exclusion–like redlining and school segregations–and finding a place where everyone feels welcome can be challenging. While not without its own history of exclusionary practices, the Park today is a backyard to many New Orleanians and its size gives it a feel of the wild in the midst of the city. Creating a space specifically for youth to grow food for their community presented a unique opportunity for both the organization and the Park.

Small Center was more than a partner to this project; it was a shepherd. The Center was then led by Scott Bernhard. Emilie Taylor Welty and Dan Etheridge made up the small but mighty team. While it's clear that the organization did an amazing job designing and constructing the farm's eco-campus, what is less obvious is all the behind-the-scenes support the Center provided to help the fledgling nonprofit launch, from visiting potential program models to connecting Grow Dat with the University's incredibly capable fundraising support, and much more.

Danish architect Jan Gehl famously said, "First life, then spaces, then buildings–the other way around never works." Design is about so much more than just buildings. Good design follows the patterns of life and makes it better at many scales. Small Center has played a critical role supporting the creation of social infrastructure, like

// BELOW: Grow Dat's boardwalk entrance. Photo: Will Crocker

the Grow Dat eco-campus, that follows the ethos of New Orleans. The city is made great not by one incredible musician, but by thousands. The city is made great not by one gorgeous building, but by streets of colorful, vibrant homes, lovingly cared for by the city's many dedicated residents.

Small Center has been the design team for hundreds of entrepreneurs, culture-bearers, educators, neighborhood leaders, and everyday residents who create the city's richness. Bringing the practical skills of design and construction to Grow Dat resulted in a beautiful and functional indoor/outdoor eco-campus where young adults take classes, process harvested produce to sell at market, learn to cook, and build deep relationships. Today, this space is imbued with the positive memories of hundreds of young adults who have learned new skills and gained a new sense of themselves while spending time there. Small Center has made this corner of City Park a beloved place. This was done not through the magic of designing against a blank canvas, but the opposite: through the beautiful and dynamic challenge of taking what already exists and amplifying it, making the whole greater than the sum of the parts.

Engagement as Practice

Bahareh Rana Javadi

The former Small Center student and intern reflects on finding her calling in public interest design.

My interest in architecture has never been about buildings, but about people. I grew up in Chicago, where I learned to love the city and how people animate public space in a way that buildings alone cannot. As a young architecture student, I knew I wanted to pursue a career in public interest design but had little intention of becoming an architect. I was inspired by design activists like Emily Pilloton and Matthew Miller, who started a design-build program at a rural high school in Bertie County, North Carolina, and Yashar Hanstad's work with the Makoko community, using local building and weaving techniques to design and build a floating school in Lagos, Nigeria. Instead of internships at architecture firms, I spent my summers fundraising and organizing for public interest research groups and environmental campaigns in Chicago. I spent my spring breaks volunteering with Habitat for Humanity to build affordable housing in Mississippi, Global Environmental Brigades to build a green house in Panama, and Global Architecture Brigades to build a school in Honduras.

// OPPOSITE: Woven driftwood art at the Pyramid Institute. Photo courtesy Bahareh Javadi
// ABOVE: New Orleans residents gather to discuss the master plan for City Park

I moved to New Orleans in 2012 to continue my study of public interest design at Tulane as a graduate student. New Orleans expanded my interests to include not only how people activate designed space, but also the informal and spontaneous ways that people transform public space. I discovered a DIY skatepark underneath the interstate, was invited to join second-line parades that took over the street, and watched people use the neutral ground as a public park. At Tulane, I made it my focus to embrace and advocate for this ground-up placemaking in my design practice. I had tremendous opportunities to immerse myself in this work. I used a travel fellowship to document examples of guerrilla urbanism in fourteen American cities. I worked with the Pyramid Resources Wellness Institute's residents to design a driftwood art piece as a backdrop to their courtyard in a Small Center Design-Build studio, and I prototyped tactical urban furniture that invited participation from the community. I sought any opportunity to incorporate community participation into my design projects. After graduating in 2014, I worked with former professor Marcella Del Signore and the Downtown Development District to launch the inaugural Park(ing) Day in New Orleans. We, along with colleagues and friends, built an interactive parklet for the event.

Still intent on not working at a traditional architecture firm, I spent my first year with two architecture degrees teaching art and design enrichment classes to K-12 students and freelancing for former professors and local organizations in New Orleans. I worked with my friend, Jose Cotto, and the New Orleans Arts Council to build the Youth Solutions design curriculum. Now operating as the Arts New Orleans' Young

Artist Movement, this design curriculum teaches youth art, design, and leadership skills while creating public art and placemaking in their communities. Through this work I was introduced to Concordia. They were the first firm that did not question my meandering resume or whether I wanted to be an architect in my interview. I joined the Concordia team in 2015 and still haven't found a place I'd rather practice.

I have worked on a wide range of projects at Concordia, including perimeter fence and sidewalk replacements, school parking lot and awning additions, private residences, restaurants, breweries, yoga studios, school renovations, police stations, natatoriums, recreation centers, public park master plans, educational master plans, community resilience and relocation plans, youth engagement plans, curriculum designs, public market studies, and planned developments. Some projects are more glamorous than others – but every project serves the public good. I used to think of public interest design as a certain kind of project, with a certain kind of client, but my professional experience over the last decade has taught me that it is a philosophy and practice that can be applied to any project type, for any client. My practice is not focused on merely providing solutions. It is rooted in empowering others with the tools to co-create solutions with me. These days, I am less concerned with branding my work as public interest design. At the end of the day, I want to use my knowledge and skills to do good work with good people, contribute positively to my community and the planet, and listen and learn with an open heart and mind.

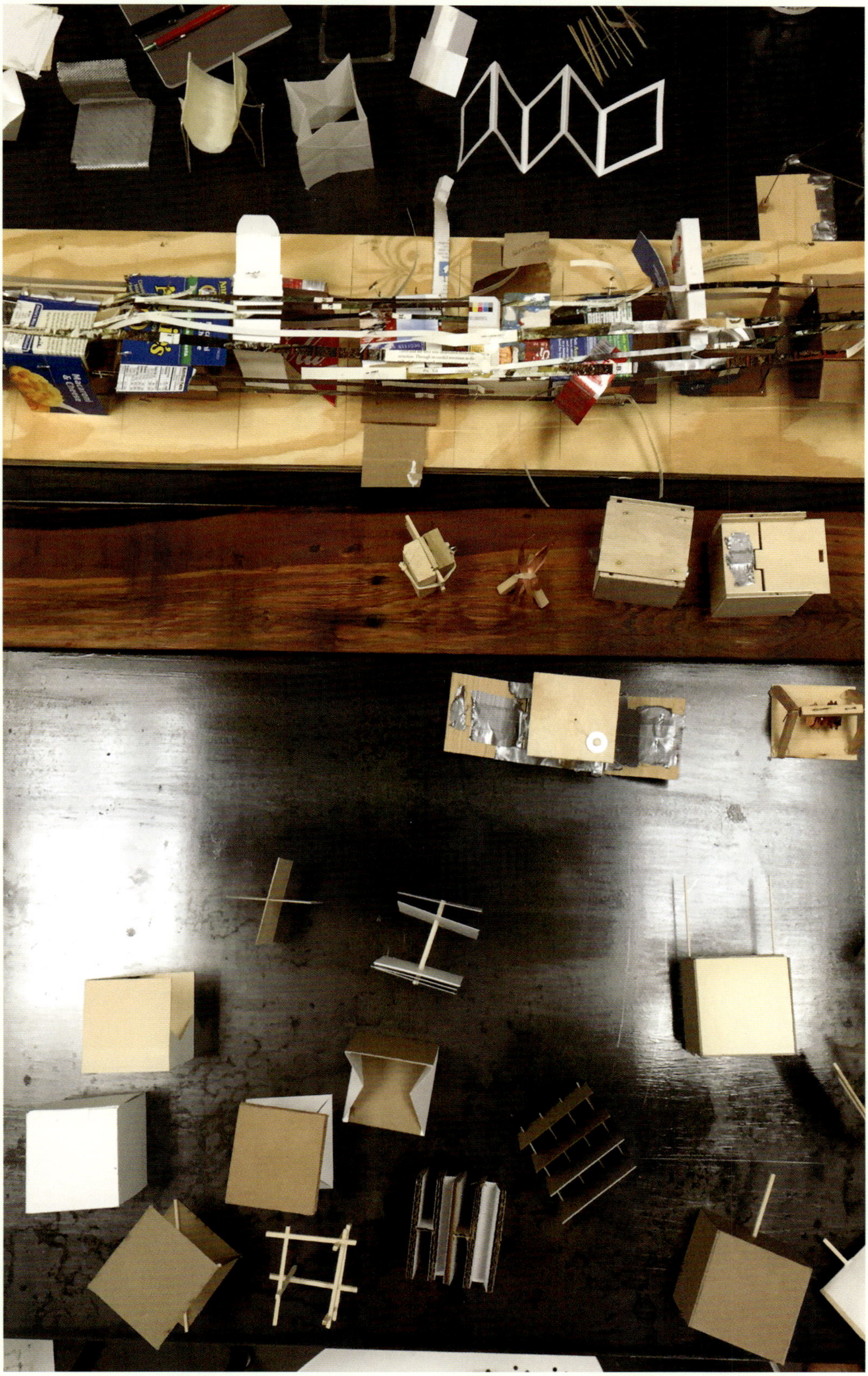

4

Amplifying Knowledge on the Ground

"Students learn the ideal of deep engagement where subject matter knowledge and lived experience are both seen as critical inputs to the design process."

Small Center's work relies on expertise from many disciplines and elevates lived experience as an essential part of understanding place. To take in the context of each design project, students, staff, and faculty must spend time listening, asking questions, and getting to know the everyday rhythms of the communities within which they work. This includes building dynamic, interdisciplinary teams to ensure that the appropriate range of experts, including a project's eventual users, are at the table in equal standing. Small Center has worked for twenty years to continually connect to the depth of knowledge on the ground. The Center builds unique teams for each project, convening interdisciplinary expertise tailored to the needs of a given project's focus or topic. Necessarily, much of that expertise comes from project partners themselves, their networks, and their constituents.

Small Center is also dedicated to educating the next generation of thoughtful designers and advocates for New Orleans's future. Students are taught to value the ideal of deep engagement, where subject matter knowledge and lived experience are both critical inputs to the design process. However, students also learn the limitations of relying on data and design alone to steward change. The projects in this chapter illustrate how knowledge on the ground often challenges preconceptions and reshapes conversations about how design might contribute to change. The Center and its project teams bring design expertise to the table but remain flexible and responsive even when design is not needed as the first step, or even the primary driver, of a project.

Students working on Small Center projects are asked to volunteer with partner organizations. This is done to foster a spirit of service, but it also affords firsthand observation of the nonprofit's functions, needs, and constituencies. Informal input can also be gathered as students work alongside, with, and for a local nonprofit and its members or clientele. Many people do not feel comfortable sharing their design preferences or general experiences in formal meetings. To address this, Small Center holds a variety of gathering types designed to be accessible to a wide range of people whose ages, jobs, or other factors determine their ability to participate at certain times, places, or meeting types. Volunteering allows students to understand the work of the partner organization, observe existing spatial dynamics, imagine alternatives, and hear directly from other volunteers, staff members, or clients about their visions for possible change.

During a meeting to discuss recovery from Hurricane Katrina, the mayor of a small city on the gulf coast once told a Small Center staff member, "The next planner that comes into town, I'm going to shoot." Perhaps hyperbolic–though perhaps not!–the statement captures a sentiment pervasive in New Orleans and many post-disaster communities; they saw resources and outside volunteers focused on recovery planning, but there was often little to no coordination with potential federal or philanthropic funding. In short, many plans were drawn up, input gathered, and dreams envisioned, but then not much happened. Even twenty years into the city's recovery, Small Center is conducting architectural design and planning projects in an atmosphere of "planning fatigue." This reinforces the need to engage first and ensure the project's scope and design tasks are suited to purpose and co-developed with community members. The Center engages students in project budgeting, material purchasing, and other practical aspects of every design project. But just as important are internal team workshops to shape engagement questions, ensuring that the materials the Center disseminates provide transparency to participants about available funding and project timelines.

Working on Small Center projects, students learn a variety of methods for engagement, from designing different meeting types to framing questions broad enough to be accessible and specific enough to solicit valuable insights. This is part of the process of learning to engage with intent; rather than conducting "check the box" outreach, engagement results must be analyzed at each stage and help shape the direction of the design process thereafter. Even before a project's design phase begins, students' design skills are well-utilized in creating visual preference surveys, presenting site analysis, or creating schematic design options for public meetings. Illustration is often used as a means of grounding engagement conversations in reality. Students provide large-scale site maps and other contextual parameters, initially without presenting any design ideas. This allows for public meeting or focus group participants to look at, draw, and imagine the project together, free to suggest a host of possible design ideas, while grounded by context and realistic constraints.

Small Center is valued in New Orleans for having been consistently accessible. Unconstrained by the academic calendar, its year-round presence allows students to take on more ambitious projects. Project timelines are often delayed by circumstances outside a designer's control, such as unforeseen regulatory hurdles, delays in material delivery, and extended periods of rain. Full-time staff can address these issues to complete past projects and develop the time-intensive setup for new ones, including engaging with partners and their constituents outside of the narrow curricular timeframe of a semester or summer fellowship. However, the bulk of Small Center's projects take place during the academic year because including students, starting in the research and design of public meetings, meets a critical pedagogical goal. It can teach students to recognize the value of on-the-ground knowledge, allow them to design creative engagement methods, and train them to parse the disparate wants and needs gleaned from the engagement process. In evaluation surveys of past Center projects, nonprofit partners have praised the commitment of Tulane architecture students. Small Center believes this dedication stems from first-hand experience: direct participation in the engagement process, volunteering, and informal interaction with the communities the project serves. The hope is that, even in significantly different project settings, whether at traditional architecture firms or other design and development entities, students will bring to their professional careers a passion for tailoring designs and design processes to the real needs of their clients.

A project partner praised the seriousness with which Tulane students considered the input of its high school students, gathered over a recurring series of in-school lunch meetings throughout the design process to bring youth perspectives to a design that would serve their needs. This responsiveness came naturally to Tulane students since they were just a few years older than the high schoolers, but also because they were involved in designing the project's comprehensive engagement process. All of this direct participation and training is in service of teaching students to respond to stakeholder input in real time. Small Center partners have noted the openness and fluidity of the Center's engagement process, responding to needs as they arise. Partners can help define the stakeholders for their project and decide how to engage them. Outlined in this chapter are projects in which community input trumped architectural design, preliminary graphic designs were revealed to be wildly off-message, and a design-build project spurred a public information campaign. Each pivot was guided by engagement inputs and provided lessons for Small Center team members and nonprofit partners alike, resulting in enduring impacts.

ADVOCACY

Cornerstones

Preserving Places of Cultural Heritage, 2008

The federal levee failure and flood following Hurricane Katrina destroyed tens of thousands of homes and gathering spaces across New Orleans. Beyond the physical damage, 100,000 Black people were displaced from New Orleans, and with them their stories, social networks, and personal histories. As recovery efforts picked up, and demographics changed rapidly across the city, there was an additional threat to the people, places, and culture that defined New Orleans.[31] Small Center worked to support existing cultural entities by physically rebuilding some of the damaged properties and cultural institutions. But, often, the needed work consisted of documentation and visioning, recognizing the cultural significance of everyday places in a public way. It was critical to expand the definition of what was deemed architecturally significant in the city and document key neighborhood anchors as a means of advocating for their preservation.

Working with the Neighborhood Story Project and preservationist Bethany Rodgers, Small Center helped produce the book, *Cornerstones: Celebrating the Everyday Monuments and Gathering Places of New Orleans Neighborhoods,* which pays homage to seven local landmarks from bars and restaurants to backyard museums and barbershops. Through interviews, site mapping, architectural drawings, and photos, the publication illustrates the range of ways these specific sites, and neighborhood places in general, are important to New Orleans. As part of the book release New Orleanians were encouraged to nominate additional "community cornerstones" that told the story of their community or served as neighborhood landmarks.

Recognizing and celebrating neighborhood gathering places proved the need for collaborative storytelling and collective input. Often humble buildings that would not be identified as significant in a traditional analysis were named by neighbors as important cultural spaces for musicians, working class residents, Black social aid and pleasure clubs, and others. The project put a spotlight on neighborhood bars that serve as an extension of the neighborhood, barbershops that are hubs of after-school activity, and clubs that some of the oldest membership organizations the city calls home and considers sacred. The project and its framework prompted an academic and professional dialogue about what the work of preservationists should, and could, entail.

Small Center conducted surveys of the locally identified cornerstone locations, including photographic documentation and architectural drawings. The project team visited during regular business hours for ethnographic observations and formal and informal interviews, and conducted historic records research. Newly named cornerstones were celebrated with a neighborhood party and postcard series, and these nominations populated a new Cornerstones website.

Documentation and publication can serve to secure the legacy of neighborhood cultural institutions, provide materials for fundraising towards economic recovery or renovation, or simply preserve local stories of place for posterity. They also serve

"It's not just about the buildings. It's about the people."

to amplify the reach of such stories, and Small Center's work has often snowballed in this way with new projects building on prior relationships. After the publication of *Cornerstones*, the team was asked by community members to document and position the significance of the Candlelight Lounge within the historic Tremé neighborhood and greater New Orleans so that efforts to sustain the barroom might find support. The Candlelight Lounge was the only long-standing barroom and live music venue still open in the Historic Tremé, a community celebrated for its jazz and performance culture.

The Cornerstones project also documented other sites in New Orleans with an uncertain future, such as the Mother-In-Law Lounge, after the owner's passing, and the Deutsches Haus in Lower Mid-City, prior to its demolition for the development of a new hospital and biomedical complex. Cornerstones documents presented a portrait of places that served a significant daily role in the lives of New Orleans residents, past and present. The goal was to recognize internationally celebrated institutions which sustain the performance culture that defines New Orleans, but that are often overlooked for traditional funding. This required an interdisciplinary project team and extensive engagement with businesses and residents to ensure the effort captured the true essence of the places and spaces held dear by each neighborhood.

[31] Elizabeth Fussell, Narayan Sastry, and Mark VanLandingham, "Race, socioeconomic status, and return migration to New Orleans after Hurricane Katrina," *Population and environment* 31, nos. 1-3 (2010): 20-42, https://doi.org/10.1007/s11111-009-0092-2.

BUILD

Pyramid Wellness Institute

Creating Space for Healing, 2012

A Small Center design-build studio examined issues surrounding mental illness in New Orleans by engaging with the staff and clients of the Pyramid Resources Wellness Institute (PRWI). Research shows that one in six New Orleanians have mental health issues which impact their daily lives.[32] Many public funding sources established to meet this need have been cut, leaving gaps in mental health services (see the Behavioral Health & Schools project later in this chapter). PRWI helps to address these service gaps by providing housing and a day center for New Orleanians with mental health challenges, including treatment services for the unhoused population and those with mental illness diagnoses or co-occurring substance use and mental illness.

Small Center's design team was asked to transform a common outdoor space into an area suited to the multiple needs of residents: group meetings, outdoor dining,

conflict resolution, activity space, and a calming oasis for both facility clients and staff. The project repurposed a liminal alley, elevating its restrictive dimensions into a vibrant and functional place. Flexible seating, vegetation, and a protective canopy created shade and enclosure, adding functionality to the main facility without the expense of additional conditioned space.

Small Center students and faculty worked collaboratively with the nonprofit's organizers and residents to create designs that incorporated each of their voices. Students informed their designs with information from both mental health treatment specialists and those experiencing mental health challenges. Residents attended student-led workshops to co-create designs for the site, and they worked together to collect pieces of driftwood along New Orleans' river levees, engraving them with residents' favorite motivational phrases. Hearing directly from clients and residents of Pyramid allowed the team to understand the daily challenges associated with addiction and mental health conditions, and to design an intervention aligned closely with the stated needs and concerns of the residents.

Hearing and experiencing this on-the-ground knowledge through an inclusive engagement process was critical to the creation of a space well-suited to gathering, fellowship, and relaxation. The project served the organization's residents and daily clients, but also community fundraising events and cookouts connecting the organization to the broader New Orleans population. The design aimed to make space for connections between residents, community members, and staff, following the central tenets of compassion, empathy, and understanding the needs of others.

As seen in previous chapters, Small Center design-build projects include significant research on project partners' work, associated scholarship from the field, and in-person learning from experts. Students working on the Pyramid Wellness project were struck by the depth of the challenges faced by the organization and the limitations of an architectural intervention in addressing complex social issues. In response to state funding cuts for mental health resources, they initiated a graphic advocacy campaign. They volunteered their faces to populate a poster and sticker series showing that such issues could affect anyone, widening the impact of the design-build project with an associated public awareness campaign.

[32] Mollyann Brodie et al., *New Orleans Five Years After the Storm: A New Disaster Amid Recovery*, (The Henry J. Kaiser Family Foundation, 2010), https://www.kff.org/wp-content/uploads/2013/02/8089.pdf.

// BELOW Architectural drawings and renderings allow the design team to convey and collaboratively develop plans and material details.

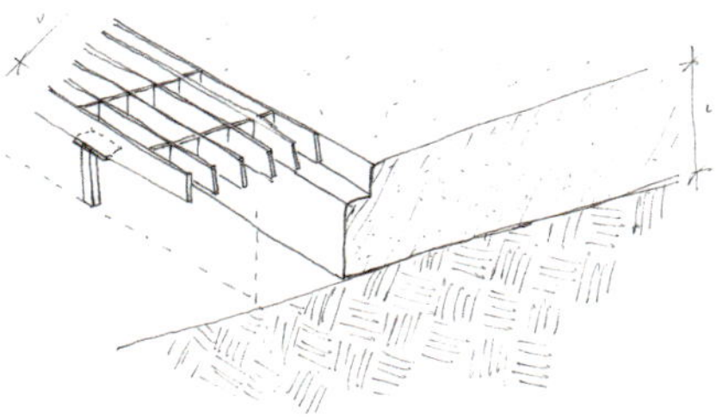

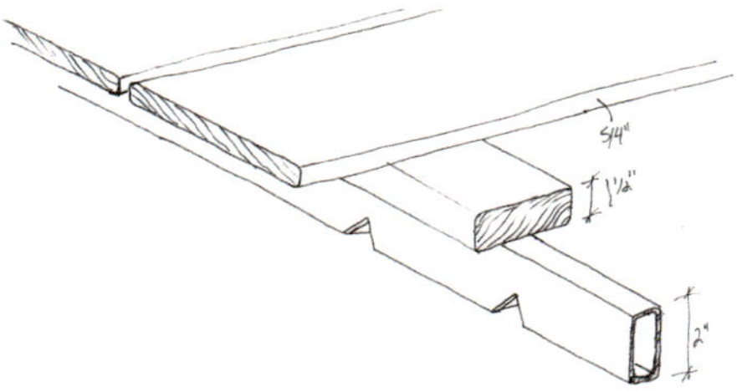

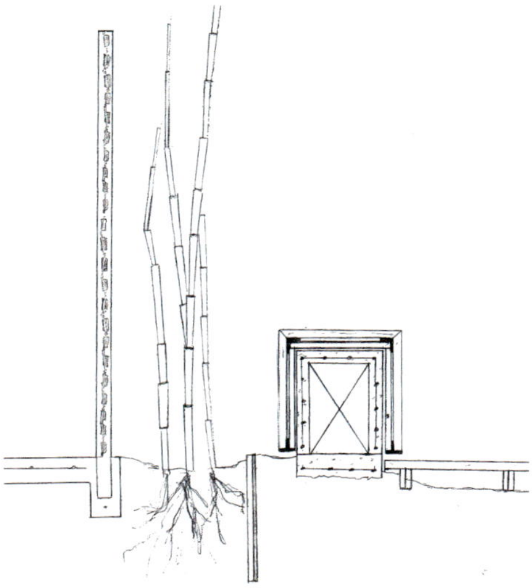

// ABOVE: Pyramid staff and clients helping to plant and enjoying the new gathering space.

ADVOCACY

Guide to Street Performance

Visualizing Musicians' Rights, 2015

Since 2013, Small Center has offered Public Interest Design (PID) Fellowships during the summer months. The Fellowship provides opportunities for students to engage with Small Center projects and partners full time. The commitment of selected students and the Fellowship's concentrated timeframe create opportunities for deep engagement and rapid results. In 2015, Small Center and its PID Fellows worked with the Music and Culture Coalition of New Orleans (MaCCNO) to create a pocket guide to regulations for street performance in the French Quarter and the Marigny. The idea was to provide clarity for both musicians and law enforcement regarding confusing rules governing performance volume and allowable locations that had often been misunderstood and wrongly enforced.

Representing local musicians, MaCCNO shared complaints received from its members that a lack of clarity about the laws governing street performance (by musicians,

neighborhood groups, and enforcement agencies alike) lead to misunderstandings, incorrectly issued citations, and loss of income for performers. Recognizing the importance of this New Orleans tradition, Small Center and MaCCNO collaborated to develop a tool that would offer unbiased information about the laws. The project began with a series of interviews with subject matter experts and was followed with group interviews of musicians representing the brass band and street musician communities. These discussions changed the work from an overarching examination of the noise ordinance to a deeper dive into the regulations governing street performance in downtown New Orleans. The design team took to the streets of the French Quarter, spending several nights conducting interviews with street musicians and confirming that a lack of knowledge about regulations on allowable locations and volume was a significant problem.

After an initial round of research and design, MaCCNO and key participants from the initial interviews were invited to review a draft of a foldable, pocket-size graphic guide. Another review with representatives from the Mayor's Office of Cultural Economy brought clarification of several pending regulatory changes. A final charrette at a local venue drew musicians, performers, activists, and attorneys for additional feedback.

One of the key challenges for MaCCNO was a broad perception that there was no regulation currently in place, and confusion as to which regulations applied where and to whom. In supporting MaCCNO's advocacy work through this project, Small Center's role was to create an accurate, accessible tool that was neutral in content and tone to reach multiple audiences. The design team's fresh perspective and graphic representation helped to clarify critical issues and resulted in a visual tool that challenged perceptions of lawlessness through an examination of the many regulations in effect.

The guide was useful in reframing conversations with the Department of Health and others around the need for greater clarity in regulations and more equitable enforcement. Thousands of copies were made available to musicians and interested patrons at local venues as a pocket reference. Small Center subsequently learned that a digital copy was loaded onto the iPads of the French Quarter Task Force as a reference tool to better understand the regulations.

This iterative approach to engagement sought a diversity of expertise with different perspectives on, and experiences with, the issue of street performance. It was equally important to engage with the various constituent groups both before and throughout the process, given that design proposals often spark new lines of thinking that may not have been considered in earlier information gathering phases. Legible graphic design arguably has some universal principles, but experience proves that target audiences must be consulted to tease out subjective differences in perception and understanding. Small Center and MaCCNO's networks provided these opportunities, and the project team's insistence on engagement and reengagement led to wide adoption of the tool.

// OPPOSITE: The foldable graphic guide to street performance.
//BELOW: MaCCNO leadership and students preview an early version of the guide.

ADVOCACY

Behavioral Health & Schools

Mapping Data to Help Students, 2016

Small Center's work with educational institutions has included a wide range of design projects, from those co-built with high school students to those that end in neighborhood planning and visioning exercises. It is important to engage with young New Orleanians for the same reasons as any other constituency; amongst these, expertise in experiencing the built environment is hyper-local and can be generation specific. Across all Small Center projects, youth voices have provided some of the most colorful, straightforward, and creative ideas during the collaborative design process. Embedding design ideas that orient a given project to the needs of young people unfailingly brings humor, joy, and a much-needed focus on the future.

// ABOVE: Small Center fellows used GIS to overlay patient locations with mental healthcare providers.
// OPPOSITE: School board members and other constituents gathered to provide feedback.

New Orleans faces higher levels of mental and behavioral health challenges than the national average, including amongst youth.[33] The city also has the highest percentage of charter schools in the United States (nearly one hundred percent).[34] This decentralized education model presents a number of challenges, including the loss of schools as neighborhood anchors and the difficulty of coordinating behavioral health services and treatment within and around each school.

As part of a Public Interest Design Seminar and in collaboration with the New Orleans Recovery School District, Small Center mapped the similarly decentralized school and behavioral health systems in order to understand gaps in care and suggest improved access for all public-school students. Through GIS mapping, students explored the spatial relationships among schools, youth programming, and city-wide transit systems. The studies revealed various issues related to New Orleans' post-Katrina school system, including a lack of reliable transportation and limited access to health services and recreation opportunities. Building upon the seminar-based work, Small Center's summer Public Interest Design Fellows assessed gaps in order to suggest future placement of services and needed policy changes. What resulted was a graphic document with maps and analysis showing the proximity of clinics to schools, the types of treatment offered and insurance accepted, and the languages clinic staff speak. The document was used to advocate for equitable distribution of services through a more centralized behavioral health system for New Orleans public school students.

Throughout the effort, Small Center drew upon its own network and that of the public school system to better understand current healthcare needs. The team engaged with teachers, students, parents, and administrators as experts in both providing and receiving such health services. In this case, a lack of response from private behavioral healthcare providers throughout the project shed light on where communication failures and the absence of a public-interest mandate create issues in the provision of consistent quality care across the city. Only local students and parents could speak to the challenges they faced and assess possible solutions, making them the critical driving voices of the project.

---

[33] Stephen W. Phillippi, Saskia Vos, and Kaylin Beiter, *Louisiana Behavioral Health Provider Survey of Youth Related Services* (LSUHSC School of Public Health, 2017).

[34] Jamie M. Carroll et al., *A New First: From State Takeover to the Nation's First All-Charter, District-Governed School System in New Orleans* (Education Research Alliance for New Orleans, 2024).

//OPPOSITE: Students brainstorm research and visual representation methods.
// TOP: Tulane students partnered with Groundwork New Orleans students to perform door-to-door surveying.
//ABOVE: The final booklet allowed the school board to present findings to school administrators citywide.

Renters' Advocacy

Supporting Affordable and Safe Housing, 2016

Small Center has gained legitimacy and built trust over twenty years of operation by collaborating closely with people and organizations working on the most pressing challenges facing New Orleans. Housing is one of those issues. The Center has tackled housing challenges with a variety of partners through graphic advocacy projects, built housing, exhibits, and public programming that shed light on housing-related economic and policy issues. In 2016, Small Center worked with the Greater New Orleans Fair Housing Action Center (GNOFHAC) to create graphic tools informing residents about rental housing conditions in the city to support their efforts for greater protections for renters. Organizations like GNOFHAC respond to the concerns of individual residents, and learning from this kind of grassroots representation has enriched Small Center design projects. While it is critical to engage with both partners and their constituencies throughout any design process, such efforts are made even more successful when building upon the work

// BELOW & OPPOSITE: Small Center gathered a wide range of constituents to discuss project goals and select from schematic graphic advocacy designs created by students.

of professional organizers and issue advocates like GNOFHAC. Such collaborations also yield long-term partnerships that benefit both Small Center and its partners; as new challenges arise, networks of nonprofits and institutional partners can build on past efforts and come together anew.

Though the 2008 recession was somewhat muted in New Orleans due to the presence of disaster recovery money following Hurricane Katrina, the hurricane also shifted the city from one of relative affordability to one with skyrocketing housing prices.[35] Louisiana's generally landlord-friendly laws exacerbated matters with short eviction notice standards and little oversight. Many New Orleans renters live in unsafe conditions which directly impact their health, productivity, and quality of life.

GNOFHAC sought to build support for legislation requiring the inspection and enforcement of safe rental housing. Small Center led a collaboration to develop and test graphic materials through a series of iterations, interviews, and focus groups that identified biases in perceptions of housing conditions and renter demographics. In supporting GNOFHAC's advocacy work through this project, the Center's role was to create accurate and engaging tools that were informative and would reframe the conversation about housing by focusing on health and safety in a city where fifty-three precent of residents are renters and have few protections or regulations for housing.

Students, faculty, and staff created engaging graphic materials, including a postcard series highlighting unsafe rental housing conditions and alerting recipients to possible remedies. Combining statistics on the percentage of rental housing that lacks basic plumbing or is rodent-infested with narratives from GNOFHAC's clients put a human face on the issues while providing a sense of the problem's scale. Engagement with local renters was critical to shaping messaging, but also provided an important check on the design process. While reviewing possible graphics and text for the campaign featuring renters in precarious building conditions, one focus group said strongly and unanimously that they were "tired of seeing people like us in 'downtrodden' positions." They suggested that graphics focusing on precise housing challenges, whether mold or lack of functional utilities, rather than the renters themselves, would make a stronger campaign without perpetuating negative stereotypes of, in this case, Black women.

Small Center also created a printed mailer that recipients could cut out and assemble into a 3D house, that also highlighted rental quality issues. The Center designed and constructed a life-sized version of this house that was assembled as a walk-in pop-up at various events around the city. A parallel advocacy effort was mailed out to 4,000 households in Fall 2016. Impacts of these efforts included a shift in media coverage of rental conditions and regulations, as well as legislation in New Orleans City Council in support of a rental registry and increased housing inspections, now a reality.[36]

Projects like those above demonstrate the limitations of design alone. Small Center students, faculty, and staff bring their own expertise as designers, as residents of New Orleans, as renters and homeowners, and some as New

// ABOVE & OPPOSITE: Postcards and mailers were created to aid the nonprofit partner's advocacy campaign.

Orleans natives. Design tools are used to visualize on-the-ground knowledge. This represents a counterpoint to top-down approaches to public policy, in which best practices are often borrowed from cities with very different politics, cultural histories, and environmental conditions. However, without gathering collaborators with diverse perspectives, backgrounds, and areas of expertise, it is impossible to fully inform any engaged design project.

---

[35] Kelly Mellott, "Cost of Housing in New Orleans Increases 33% After Katrina says HUD," *Housingwire*, September 29, 2010, https://www.housingwire.com/articles/cost-of-housing-in-new-orleans-increases-33-after-katrina-says-hud/#:~:text=The%20first%20survey%20of%20its,2004%20to%20%24882%20in%202009.

[36] Patrick Daurio, "Healthy Homes Rental Registry Program sets new standard for N.O. rentals," on WWLTV, June 17, 2024, 3 min., 50 sec., https://www.wwltv.com/video/news/local/morning-show/289-1061b9e3-8402-409e-8650-e9a9b95c380f.

Fighting for Safe Housing Rights

Maxwell Ciardullo

The nonprofit policy director and Small Center partner discusses the critical nature of getting advocacy messaging pitch perfect to ensure inclusivity and effectiveness amongst both policy-makers and those whose challenges are being represented.

When I joined the Louisiana Fair Housing Action Center's (LaFHAC) policy team in 2014, we were already two years into an effort to pass basic health and safety protections for New Orleans renters. That work started in 2012 when the organization partnered with national researchers to understand how other cities were addressing this problem and issued a "white paper" on a model policy for New Orleans. What eventually became law in November 2022 was, for the most part, fully present in that white paper a decade earlier. It was full of charts, graphs, important data, and model programs, which are all important in this kind of advocacy, but it was individual renters' knowledge and experiences that ultimately resulted in passage of an ordinance. LaFHAC's partnership with Small Center on this campaign began in 2016.

What we eventually called our Healthy Homes Campaign was also born out of the experiences of the organization's clients. LaFHAC is a statewide nonprofit fair housing center based in New Orleans. At the time, it provided direct services to our clients in the form of pro bono representation for victims of housing discrimination, as well as foreclosure prevention counseling. However, as one of the higher-profile housing organizations in the city, its intake staff were regularly flooded with calls from renters stuck in homes with dangerous health and safety violations. One of the most memorable from my early days was an older, visually impaired woman who often used her hands to feel for the walls and orient where she was in her home. She was calling about what she first thought was water dripping down her walls from the unit above her, but that she quickly discovered was raw sewage. Her landlord was refusing to make repairs and she was desperate for help.

In cases like this, staff referred people to the local legal aid organization, but we all knew there was little any organization could do to help. That's largely because Louisiana's–and most states'–renter protections are abysmal. Sure, it violates health and safety codes to have sewage dripping down your walls, but what good are those codes if there's no one to enforce them, as had been the case in New Orleans for years. Even if the code enforcement staff were available, complaining about your landlord is a surefire way to get evicted, and Louisiana doesn't have protections against retaliation. It was the staff's anger and inability to help in cases like this that motivated us to launch the Healthy Homes Campaign.

We collaborated with Small Center at the same time as we were working with city councilmembers to introduce a Healthy Homes ordinance. In order to build visible support for the ordinance, we needed outreach and advocacy materials that would resonate with renters dealing with substandard conditions. The Center and its summer fellows helped us organize focus groups and design a brochure and mailer. In the last focus group, one of our participants correctly called out what we anticipated would be the final design for the mailer for relying on the trope of a low-income Black woman as a victim, lacking agency. The rest of the group agreed, and for me it was a humbling reminder to ensure the people closest to the problem are involved in crafting the solutions.

Small Center staff and fellows also had the bright idea of taking the brochure, which they designed to be folded into the shape of a house, and building a fourteen-foot-tall foam board version. Once constructed, people could walk inside and out and read statistics about the number of renter households that dealt with mold or rats in the last year, as well as quotes and stories from individual renters. Aside from just being

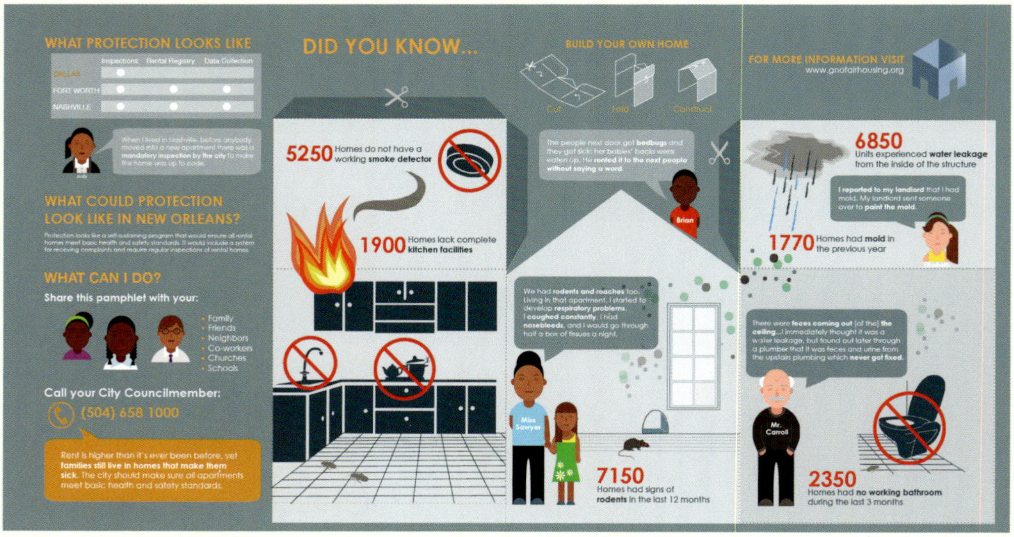

very cool to look at, the foam board house also helped us solve an important problem we were experiencing with the media.

When LaFHAC's clients were interested, we would often try to pitch their stories of dealing with negligent landlords to the press in hopes the attention would create pressure to secure repairs. Unfortunately, many local news agencies had their own biases and often believed landlords over our disproportionately low-income Black renter clients. It became clear that, if we wanted to create an opportunity for our clients to tell their own stories without being defamed by their landlords, we needed to create our own press event. The first public hearing on our Healthy Homes ordinance provided the opportunity, and the foam board house provided the perfect backdrop for our press conference outside City Hall. Dozens of renters and supporters showed up, and the stories that ran did a much better job of featuring their perspectives.

That first hearing on the Healthy Homes Ordinance was a success, but the full City Council didn't take it up again until 2022. In the meantime, it was the knowledge of LaFHAC's clients and renters participating in the local tenant's union that greatly improved the ordinance, adding anti-retaliation protections and help for renters facing displacement because of health and safety violations. Unfortunately, the City Council made significant concessions to the landlord lobby before the ordinance's final passage, but the new law still offers assistance and protection to thousands of families.

Where Recovery Took Root

Austin Allen

The landscape architect and Center for Sustainable Engagement and Development board member discusses how community-based design initiatives in the Lower 9th Ward have created opportunities for residents to bring local expertise to resilience planning.

The City Center's founding was rooted in the difficult recovery years from 2005 through 2009, where the survival of the Lower Ninth Ward was often questioned by many outside agencies, entities, and individuals, but never doubted by hopeful residents. Thousands of volunteers up for the challenge committed to build a new reality, confronting national, regional, and local infrastructure failure along with a rapidly changing climate.

I had made my way down from the University of Colorado at Denver, where our College of Architecture and Planning had made a commitment to assist in the recovery efforts in the Lower Ninth Ward. During the four years I was a landscape architecture professor, I spent so much time in the New Orleans recovery that I eventually moved to the Lower Ninth Ward and started teaching at Louisiana State University (LSU). There were many universities, nonprofits, and individuals who had done the same,

lending support throughout New Orleans and the Lower Ninth Ward. Tulane's School of Architecture and LSU's School of Landscape Architecture often collaborated to reduce the learning curve for those from outside of Louisiana attempting to make sense of an unwieldy recovery process. The community connections made across the Lower Ninth Ward were extensive.

Pam Dashiell, then president of the Holy Cross Neighborhood Association (HCNA), was one of the first people I met leading the recovery effort for the Lower Ninth Ward. I met many more leaders who did tremendous work tying culture to place to resiliency. All were a critical part of the Lower Ninth Ward rebounding. Dashiell, though, is a key part of the Small Center pre-history. She was passionate about rethinking an adjacent wetland area as an integral part of rebuilding the Lower Ninth Ward as a sustainable and resilient community. Enhancing her efforts were other people and organizations like Malik Rahim and the Common Ground Collective, hundreds of neighbors, and certainly key individuals from Tulane including Charles Allen III, then vice president of the HCNA and part of the Tulane University School of Public Health and Tropical Medicine; John C. Williams, architect and then president of the Tulane Alumni Association; Dr. Sarah K. Mack, then a doctoral student in Global Sustainable Resource Management at Tulane and a leader in wetlands and water management; Ann Yoachim, a Tulane University School of Public Health and Tropical Medicine graduate and later program manager, Institute on Water Resources Law & Policy, now Small Center Director; and hundreds of other dedicated New Orleanians. Pam passed away by the end of 2009, late one night at a computer, writing proposals and reports aimed at bringing back the Lower Ninth Ward. Her death made it evident that greater community infrastructure was needed and had to be built on many fronts. It would take a robust coalition like those listed here to make needed progress.

These were critical, catalytic years for forging a strong enough foundation to make a comprehensive design center for New Orleans, and for creating meaningful learning experiences for students, changing the question from "Will the Lower Ninth Ward survive?" to "How will it come back?"

Three years later, it was Maurice Cox, then Associate Dean for Community Engagement at the School of Architecture at Tulane, who, when discussing the various school-led projects in the Lower Ninth Ward, would interweave the name Tulane City Center with "Small Center." I knew Cox for a number of years prior to this time. And, through many enthusiastic and intense discussions in 2013 and 2014, was moved to witness Cox's and the Center's intent on making a significant impact upon recovery efforts in the Lower Ninth. At first, I thought "small" was an adjective Cox was using, a word meant to either downplay Tulane's efforts, or, more likely, keep me focused on the capacity and scale of projects and away from asking for way too much from the Center. Certainly, Tulane's contributions had been tremendous since 2005, giving me even more reason to ask on behalf of the neighborhood! Eventually, I caught up with the name and began to like the double read, a generous gift from Albert and Tina Small, coupled with a way to define the powerful impact of a student/community collaborative of design-build initiatives without over-promising the outcomes. During those years, Maurice would often interact with LSU's Landscape Architecture Director Elizabeth Mossop on the necessity for greater collaborations. They were way ahead of both institutions on identifying the need. The Albert and Tina Small Center for Collaborative Design has caught hold of the spirit of cooperative efforts, tying the boundless energy and ideas of students to the real struggles of communities who envision a greater sense of responsible urbanism and an ability to respond to, and grow from, what we learn as we deal with the crisis of climate change and ongoing recovery.

Housing First

Andreanecia Morris

The Executive Director of Housing NOLA shares the importance of storytelling from a human perspective, with data to back it up, towards real policy change at the municipal level.

Today, America is a place where symbols are often more important than the causes or programs they describe. With social media and the twenty-four hour news cycle both competing for attention, we are desperate for bite-sized thoughts that don't offend or are designed to prompt a reaction–any reaction. Now more than ever, we see the power of effective narrative. After some handwringing and consternation, New Orleans accepted the fact that the city must address its affordable housing crisis and resolved to end it. Unfortunately, things have worsened as we struggle to implement policies that will help us turn from the disastrous course we are on and create new affordable housing opportunities. Despite the clear need to #PutHousingFirst, we are still struggling to consistently implement systemic and sustainable change. While there have been victories, they have been hard fought and have taken far too long.

I'm going to start by stating the obvious: working with community is hard. If you have worked to create change in places and spaces that you love, you know exactly what I

mean. From New York to Atlanta to San Francisco to New Orleans, we've all either seen positive change carried forward or catastrophic decisions made that set cities back years. The National Equity Atlas found that if all New Orleanians were paying no more than thirty percent of their income on housing, they would have an extra $513 million to spend annually on things like childcare, transportation, educational opportunities, savings, vacations, and other things to improve their lives. This is the basis of the economic argument for ending the affordable housing crisis. It is one we use in our advocacy because affordable housing is a term fraught with bias as it often brings to mind the worst kinds of stereotypes rooted in racism, sexism, and classism. Far too often, people of all economic levels reject the notion of affordable housing for all because of those biases–even if they themselves are struggling with the issue. We often discuss housing insecurity and trauma as separate but equally troubling challenges for people of color and/or those earning low wages. But we have to look deeper and entertain the notion that, for some, their personal affordable housing crisis is one of the traumas that has left lasting damage.

> "When you bring it down to the level of cells, the level of biological mechanisms, then it is about all of us. We are all equally susceptible and equally in need of help when adversity strikes. And that is what a lot of folks don't want to hear. Some want to stand back and pretend that this is just a poor-person problem." -Dr. Nadine Burke Harris, *The Deepest Well: Healing the Long-Term Effects of Childhood Adversity*, 2018

Trauma-informed care requires open-mindedness and compassion which should lead to the development and implementation of intersectional policies that deal with housing insecurity with the same veracity that one would deal with assault, abuse, and other trauma.

We are told the concept of political correctness is society's biggest problem when political correctness is simply thinking before you speak and accepting the consequences. That's all: it's one of the lessons we were supposed to learn in kindergarten. The danger of political correctness isn't the notion of considering your words' impact before you let them fly, it's the fact that no matter what side of the debate you're on, you often have a visceral reaction to an opposing point of view. Add social media to the mix, and instead of a thoughtful and honest discussion, you're inadvertently boxed into your position; even when that means you're defending the indefensible.

How do change agents respond when others experience that knee-jerk reaction to our ideas? What do we do when people flinch whenever we talk about the things that we believe matter most? Do we find a clarion voice and push through? Unfortunately, no.

More often than not, progressive policies are saddled with names that seem designed against invoking any emotion at all. Good programs that can and have changed lives are saddled with names likes Public Housing, Low Income Housing Tax Credit, Rental Registry, Housing Choice Voucher Program, and Inclusionary Zoning. Those are just a few, but there are many more. In the name of being accurate and precise, explaining all the drawbacks and pitfalls, we have forgotten to speak about the real benefits and to lead with the positive. In short, we've forgotten how to persuade. Clunky narrative gets in the way of reminding our allies, friends, and adversaries how these policies can change lives. Housing, one of our most basic rights, is an industry where many of us advocates trip over ourselves to explain the means instead of simply talking about the end: housing for all.

One the first priorities to come out of the HousingNOLA plan, New Orleans' ten-year strategy to end housing insecurity, was an honest assessment of inclusionary housing policies to determine whether they would work in New Orleans. We worked with a dozen developers and educated the community about the facts. We found that the term, while accurate, did little to inspire confidence in the proposed policy's ability to create affordable housing without direct subsidy. Would implementing a comprehensive Inclusionary Zoning policy be a hollow victory or would it be a step towards enshrining equity and the needs of New Orleanians in governing how and what we build? We knew it would be the latter, so why not say just that? With that decision, the Smart Housing Mix was born. No longer would we grapple with explaining the obvious–how does Inclusionary Housing work?–we would work to "Fix the Mix."

It is a term that speaks to the people of New Orleans who live with the challenges of its problematic housing market: a market that has the highest home costs in the region with the lowest wages. A market with an abundance of vacant land and properties but not enough to meet the needs of most of the people who live here. We wanted people to immediately understand our overall purpose, to make it easier to find housing that was affordable. It was important that we allow everyone to see themselves in the policy as it was not a one-size-fits-all strategy. The Smart Housing Mix will include voluntary density bonuses for the areas of the city that already have higher rates of affordability and mandatory inclusionary zoning, in the areas where opportunity outpaces affordability. It's intuitive, it's clever, and most importantly, it's smart.

We were fortunate to work with messaging and design professionals to think through this, and we did that because we acknowledged that we weren't simply looking to come up with a catchy name–we wanted to persuade. Sometimes we forget that even when we're right, people disagree with us for good reasons. Other times, we're so eager to accomplish the goal, we're afraid of offending. Still other times, we are transported back to when we always had to raise our hands to answer the question in class, droning on about a subject that thoroughly engaged us and no one else.

New Orleans has long struggled to provide services to its most vulnerable residents. Man-made or natural disasters hit the most vulnerable the hardest, and the current affordable housing crisis is no exception. As many of New Orleanians struggle to make ends meet, the devastation leaves thousands homeless or displaced, leads to an increase in physical and mental issues, and exacerbates existing health problems. Our special needs services system is too fragmented to address the needs of all of New Orleans' most vulnerable citizens. Individuals with special needs face many of the same issues as low-income New Orleanians: paying too much in rent or on a mortgage and living in neighborhoods with limited access to services. However, individuals with special needs also face additional barriers and require additional supportive services in order to thrive. Further, these populations are more at risk of not having safe and affordable housing options. In addition to examining issues faced by these populations, New Orleans government agencies and non-profits must collect more data and track progress with special needs groups.

We have to embrace the fact that work we do, if done correctly, will change people's lives and that THAT is the entire point. Dr. Martin Luther King, Jr. in his Nobel

Prize acceptance speech said, "I have the audacity to believe that peoples everywhere can have three meals a day for their bodies, education and culture for their minds, and dignity, equality, and freedom for their spirits." We must have no less audacity and be willing to do that clearly, distinctly and often, so people understand that we're not simply on their side, but that we propose initiatives like the Smart Housing Mix, Healthy Homes Ordinance, and the housing trust fund–so that eventually, we will #PutHousingFirst.

SECTION THREE

Prototyping New Futures

5

Cultivating Novel Partnerships and New Coalitions

"The Center's approach to coalition building aims to reinforce a sense of ownership in big conversations concerning the city."

One of Small Center's central tenets is that everyone has the right to shape the spaces in which they live, work, and play. But that is easier said than done: some communities' right to space is burdened by historic inequities like redlining and systemic racism. To work against these requires building and maintaining a strong network of partnerships, a community approach that is not novel to Small Center. In New Orleans, there are robust networks of nonprofit organizations in the arts, education, and youth recreation that have served as the backbones of neighborhoods long before Small Center was founded. Instead of competing with these existing services, the Center has often facilitated the visions of these organizations, serving as a convener and connector, providing high-quality design to groups that typically don't have access to such services.

Small Center is located in New Orleans' Central City neighborhood, just off of Oretha Castle Haley Boulevard. Formerly named Dryades Street, it featured one of the city's historic open markets and was a thriving commercial center. In the 1960s, the Congress of Racial Equality led a boycott of stores that wouldn't hire Black employees, which succeeded in expanding employment opportunities. However, in the 1970s, significant population decline due to white flight and associated disinvestment led to significant vacancies on the Boulevard for many years. Since the 1990s, educational, cultural, and arts nonprofits have filled the

corridor with vibrancy, opportunities for youth, and pedestrian activity leading to business development. From stalwart anchors like Ashé Cultural Arts Center to newer additions like the Youth Empowerment Project (YEP), local organizations have served as leading voices in neighborhood matters from cultural programming to business associations to municipal infrastructure investments.

Small Center has collaborated with many of these nonprofits, providing pro bono design and design-build services. The Center has also served as a gathering place for both nonprofit-led events and Small Center-curated programming and exhibitions. Working with Ashé, YEP, the NET Charter School, Southern Food and Beverage Museum, Blue House, Civic Studio, and others along the Boulevard has allowed the Center's team to understand the needs and common challenges of such organizations. Familiarity with the block has helped the Center curate programming and exhibitions about the issues facing the neighborhood, its organizations, and similar corridors across the city. More broadly, Small Center connects multiple social and political networks in the city. The Center, positioned in a university, working with government entities, and having an ear on the ground in the community, is a unique space in which change can be achieved outside of traditional channels. Critical to this effectiveness is the expansion and maintenance of the Center's network of partners across public, private, and nonprofit sectors. Small Center's longevity, visibility, and consistent accessibility are similarly crucial to maintaining influence and trust within community groups.

Reliability is as valuable in building project teams and issue-based coalitions as it is in supporting past design-build projects. Small Center's commitment to remaining available to past partners is a significant push back on the pressures in academic architecture programs to prioritize new initiatives and innovative design approaches over the work of maintaining long-term relationships. Consistency is particularly important in New Orleans, where resources associated with disaster-related funding have come and gone, and the work of outside design consultants concludes before its long-term impacts are apparent. Small Center's reliability and availability contrasts with community members' experiences with other, capricious consultants. The work it takes to maintain this constancy has budget implications. Small Center and the School of Architecture together bear the cost of the off-campus location and full-time staff. However, this investment is crucial, since the Center's consistent presence in the neighborhood builds trust with those it serves. Its proximity to partner organizations proves its genuine commitment to the neighborhood.

Small Center's identity as part of Tulane has sometimes proven to be a barrier to grassroots coalition-building because Tulane carries the reputation of an elite and exclusive institution. To combat this perception, Small Center has strategically relocated off-campus and hosts inclusive public programming, allowing the Center to build trust amongst community-based nonprofit project partners. Conversely, the very same institutional power dynamic that has proven challenging for Small Center on some projects has given the influence necessary to get other projects off the ground. Tulane University is one of the largest employers in New Orleans, meaning the Center can leverage the connections and influence of a major institution in a relatively small city. Institutional power has been of particular benefit for projects built on public lands, such as Grow Dat Youth Farm and the Hollygrove Greenline Water/Shade Pavilion, and those in which liability and bureaucracy can delay or deny projects, as with Parisite Skate Park, located underneath Interstate 610. In its off-campus, community-facing location, the Center intentionally tries to strike a balance between wielding the power of an institution to effect change and working collaboratively at the grass-roots level with project partners.

Novel partnerships are sometimes borne of necessity, but when interdisciplinarity is built into a project's research and collaborative design process, such partnerships can be cultivated and continued across projects and time. A number of organizations have been Small Center partners on more than one project, including Grow Dat Youth Farm, Jane Place Neighborhood Sustainability Initiative, City Park, and others, building on past collaborations to address current needs and new ideas. Similarly, issue-based coalitions have been built with past project partners working within the same field, including urban agriculture (Farmacia, Grow Dat, Sprout, Sugar Roots Farm), water management (Groundwork New Orleans, Carrollton-Hollygrove CDC, Lower Ninth Ward Center for Sustainable Engagement & Development), homelessness (Ozanam Inn, Hotel Hope, Hagar's House), and other areas. The Center's practice of engaging past partners in current projects benefits the work in multiple ways. The staff can slowly build in-house subject-matter expertise and continue to learn from prior projects to improve subsequent ones. Past partners and their networks serve as important experts and advisors on future projects. They also select new projects as Request For Proposal (RFP) jury members, review project designs in process, and are featured (and paid) as speakers at exhibit events and panel discussions. Building partnerships over time has led to long-lasting relationships, friendships, and grant and programming collaborations, and has allowed Small Center to become a key ally to New Orleans' existing and expanding network of nonprofits committed to improving the city.

These novel partnerships impact the Center's mission as an educator, since they bring Tulane students to new corners of the city. Most Tulane students are not local to New Orleans, so Small Center projects present opportunities to learn about their adopted city's history and culture. For some, working on Small Center projects begins their long-term love of the city. The students who make New Orleans home after graduating often spent part of their coursework on collaborative Small Center projects. Tulane students also learn healthy teamworking skills as key participants in project coalitions. Part of this includes working with younger students from local middle and high schools into its project engagement. As lifelong users of public spaces and places across our city, younger students often bring a refreshing honesty to project critiques and offer creative ideas without the baggage of the design canon. The work of the Center is enriched by gathering as many perspectives as possible, synthesizing ideas, and rendering them visual to move local projects closer to implementation.

Small Center's work creates a collective sense of ownership over the city, so that all people feel welcome in big conversations about public planning, zoning, or hyper-local neighborhood efforts. The Center is attentive to which participants—students or project partners—need support in learning new terminology or studying materials in advance to be able to fully participate in planning processes. The goal is to ensure everyone's input and expertise is considered and can help shape the places and spaces that impact everyday life in New Orleans.

VISIONING

L9 Vision Coalition

Grassroots Neighborhood Planning, 2013 - 2014

In 2013, local developers sought approval of redevelopment plans for the largest undeveloped parcel of high ground in New Orleans, the former Holy Cross School Campus. The developer's plans were created largely without input from neighborhood residents. Consequently, the New Orleans City Council delayed an approval vote and required an engagement process. The neighborhood association asked Small Center for assistance in conducting engagement and crafting its own design proposal to inform the development.

Small Center worked with the Holy Cross Neighborhood Association to bring together community groups. The Lower 9th Ward Vision Coalition (L9VC) was formed from these efforts. As with many projects in New Orleans, the impact of devastation from the federal levee failure during Hurricane Katrina (2005) loomed large over the process. The neighborhood had been permanently cleaved from the rest of New Orleans with the construction of the Industrial Canal (1918-23). The

// ABOVE & NEXT PAGE: L9 residents engage at a series of public meetings.

betrayal of this planning decision was heightened when that same canal's levee wall failed during Hurricane Katrina, producing a rush of flood water and near total devastation. The neighborhood experienced some of the worst flood damage and attracted international attention. Repeated attempts to repair the damage took the forms of grassroots activism, philanthropy, and disaster capitalism. Despite these efforts, much of the Lower Ninth Ward remained vacant, alongside blight and other economic development challenges.

The Holy Cross Neighborhood fared somewhat better than the rest of the Lower Ninth Ward, and eight years on from the storm even faced gentrification and affordability concerns. To avoid neighborhood sentiment being viewed as NIMBYism, representing only localized concerns from immediate neighbors, Small Center attempted to build a coalition whose vision for the redevelopment site would represent all neighborhoods of the Lower Ninth Ward and therefore hold the requisite political weight. The coalition brought together representatives from multiple nonprofits, neighborhood groups, cultural institutions, and residents across the entire Lower Ninth Ward. Organizations included The Holy Cross Neighborhood Association, A Community Voice, L9 Center for the Arts, L9 Homeowners Association, Lower 9th Ward Village, Tekrema Center for Art & Culture, and Art House on the Levee. Each gave generously of their time to design and execute an engagement process that could reach the entire neighborhood in order to demonstrate unity in its vision for the proposed development site.

More than 250 people attended five public meetings over two months, alongside smaller meetings and porch chats. Across this series of engagement activities, Small Center worked with L9VC to create three planning schemes representing the wishes of the whole neighborhood. By providing urban design, preservation, development financing, and landscape design expertise, Small Center ensured the L9VC's plans were realistic and financially feasible. The public planning process and educational workshops gave the community a voice and informed their proposal with realistic budgeting, compelling the developer to make a number of changes, including a reduction in proposed buildings' height from thirteen-stories to five, an elevation better suited to the otherwise low-density neighborhood, and assured community access to existing green spaces.

By facilitating public meetings and creating a broad-based coalition, Small Center enabled neighborhood leaders to promote their community vision for the site, working with the developer to ensure that community needs were considered. Following the community-led effort, the development proceeded with a controversial publicity campaign and eventually received approval by the City Council. The development stalled multiple times, and the site remains undeveloped. The delays have called into question the viability of preserving the historic school building at its center. Despite the care taken to build a coalition and develop a viable design, the effort ultimately failed to realize a completed project. Still, this emphasizes the importance of building such coalitions—that they may create networks ready to collaborate in shaping future proposals across the neighborhood.

BUILD

Parisite DIY Skate Park

Legitimacy for Community-built Recreation Space, 2013 - 2014, 2022

In 2010, a group of skaters got together and started a do-it-yourself skatepark at the intersection of Interstate 610 and Paris Avenue (explaining the name "Parisite"). At the time, New Orleans was a city of over 350,000 people with no official skateparks and few exterior places for kids to exercise outside of team sports leagues. Unstructured recreation areas such as skateparks allow youth to build self-confidence as they creatively interact with their environment, as well as with one another. Parisite had strong grassroots support, but, with growing popularity, this once informal public space drew the attention of city officials who questioned the legal implications of operating such a recreational space. The skaters approached Small Center for technical assistance in protecting the nascent park and design assistance in continuing its build-out underneath the large overhead infrastructure.

The Center's work began by building capacity for the young organization. Annie Frederick of New York's Hester Street Collaborative led a strategic planning and fundraising bootcamp. The skaters formed a Louisiana nonprofit corporation called Transitional Spaces, which enabled them to negotiate with City Hall. Through this process, Transitional Spaces became strong advocates for the park and not only convinced the city to declare the site an official skatepark but succeeded in getting a set of ramps placed on the site through a collaborative donation by Red Bull and Spohn Ranch.

In addition to support during this advocacy work, Small Center worked with Transitional Spaces to develop a vision for the park. The masterplan included specific designs for an entrance, signage, planting, benches and handrails to make the skatepark a welcoming community space. Planted areas were designed to address the need for stormwater catchment and filtration from highway overpass runoff. Small Center constructed the entryway and commissioned signage to provide a welcoming entrance to the park and official recognition of the space. The skatepark opened with a ribbon cutting in 2015, with Mayor Mitch Landrieu noting, "By working together we have created a unique place that can inspire our young people and give them an opportunity to stay physically active and out of trouble." After facing regulatory opposition for years, Parisite had arrived.

Typical challenges for built projects in public spaces include long-term governance and maintenance. Transitional Spaces has taken on the responsibility for keeping the skatepark clean, posting clear rules for safety, and programming official skate events. Building Parisite's capacity to function as its own nonprofit was a necessary step to get the project off the ground but it continues to be useful in the life of the park long after. The new nonprofit went on to successfully fundraise, design, and construct the next several phases of their park, including multiple skate ramps, bowls, and street skating features. The park and its design have garnered multiple awards and national attention, including a Silver Medal from

// LEFT: Volunteers help with upkeep at the skatepark.
//ABOVE: Skaters enjoy the half-pipe, one of many features at Parisite.

the prestigious Rudy Bruner Award for Urban Excellence in 2019, awarded partly in recognition of the inclusive design process. In 2022, Small Center worked with Transitional Spaces once more to plan a new phase of their long-term master plan, including food service pop-up facilities, seating, and a performance stage.

Parisite provides an example in which the Center leveraged Tulane University's networks and legal representation to legitimize a grassroots initiative. This collaborative effort featured inclusive engagement with neighbors and municipal decision-makers. Small Center's design-build work extended the park's benefits to non-skaters, and installed seating, planted trees, and devised flood mitigation. Visual representations and an organized design and engagement process allowed the project to move through regulatory approvals, albeit slowly. Building a coalition and making a long-term plan led to regulatory legitimacy for both the skatepark and Parisite as a nonprofit organization.

// *Skill, style, and planting natives at Parisite Skate Park.*

VISIONING

LaSalle Cultural Corridor

Mardi Gras Indian Campus, 2014 - 2015

The LaSalle Corridor in Central City is richly layered with historic places and events. From the early nineteenth century to the Civil Rights era, it has reflected and helped to define the Black experience in New Orleans. The narratives of LaSalle are those of reconstruction and Jim Crow, the challenges of the Civil Rights Movement in the Deep South, and the promise and limitations of public housing and the Great Society. Central City is known for its culture-bearers, including artists, musicians, and performers who got their start at the Dew Drop Inn, and the uptown tribes of the Mardi Gras Indians.

Redevelopment of the LaSalle corridor is an ongoing process, combining grassroots and top-down efforts to revitalize a unique street that features historic, cultural, and economic sites intermixed with residential lots. At its high point in the 1940s and '50s, LaSalle was a locus for Black entrepreneurs, musicians, and political and social activists. Post-Katrina redevelopment brought housing redevelopment and

other changes to the neighborhood, raising concerns about the need to preserve cultural institutions. Small Center built a coalition with private business owners, arts organizations, funders, cultural institutions, and public housing developers to highlight and promote the historic and cultural assets of the Central City neighborhood and their importance in New Orleans.

As a cultural landscape project, the design team included students and professors from the Louisiana State University Robert Reich School of Landscape Architecture and Tulane School of Architecture. The team conducted historic research, gathered stories from local residents at public meetings, and surveyed the corridor to identify possible locations for community-led development opportunities and to understand the needs of local businesses and residents. This analysis of Central City and LaSalle Street supported the creation of a "Cultural Corridor Plan" that all parties could use to promote development, inform their constituents, and raise funds for both individual and collective projects along the corridor.

From this larger effort to revitalize the historic corridor, a more focused collaboration emerged with a key constituency, the Mardi Gras Indian Council (MGIC). A revered local cultural institution, the MGIC asked Small Center for help in finding a headquarters to house their various arts and educational programming and to celebrate the culture of the uptown tribes. The Mardi Gras Indians are a treasured cultural tradition of New Orleans. Though they garner attention nationally and around the world, there are few formal spaces where their traditions can be explored as curated and presented by the Indians themselves. Further, the Mardi Gras Indians and other culture-bearers often receive accolades without receiving direct benefits from New Orleans' multi-billion-dollar tourism industry. Representing over a dozen

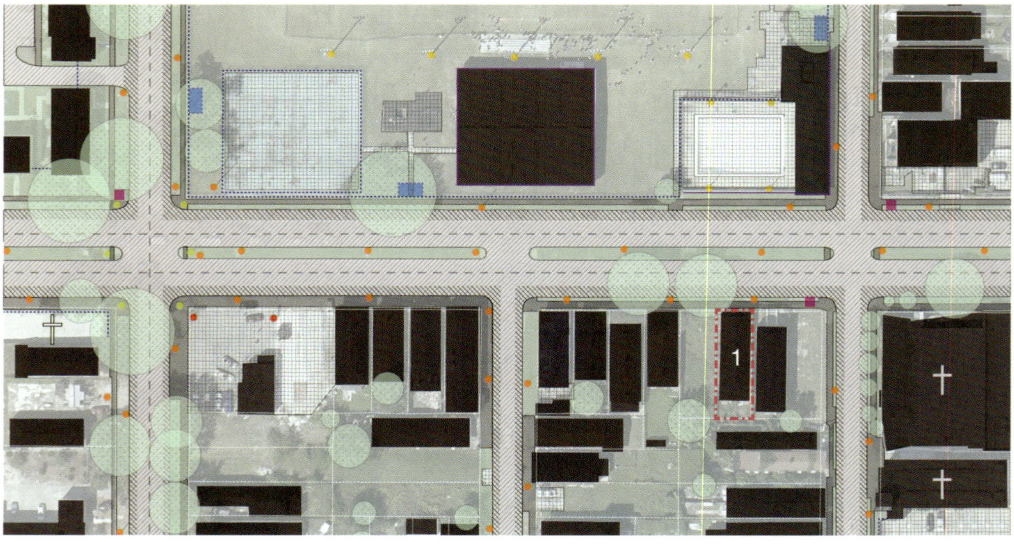

// ABOVE: LaSalle Street reimagined as an arts and cultural corridor
//LEFT: Site plan showing the Mardi Gras Indian campus in proximity to A.L. Davis Park.

tribes, the MGIC sought to create a cultural campus that would allow it to share its traditions with both the next generation of Indians and the general public.

Small Center helped develop a campus plan that combined multiple residential lots, reactivating two existing shotgun houses and creating an outdoor gathering space. The houses were reimagined as gallery, artwork storage, performance space, and multi-purpose workshop where visitors could learn sewing techniques and other skills from Mardi Gras Indian instructors. The iterative design process included assessments of a variety of possible site locations, art installations, and the design of a performance space that would allow crowds to gather during special events, such as Super Sunday and St. Joseph's Night. While Mardi Gras Indian traditions typically activate public streets and spaces with parades, masking, and performance, the campus offered a permanent home for the Indians to maintain a presence year-round.

When the project began, several new developments on the corridor had just been completed, including redeveloped public housing, a small open market, and a youth arts organization. Corridor plans are often continuous efforts, spanning years and even decades. In this case, the coalition first began as a necessary step to pursuing private and philanthropic funding. The coalition expanded existing networks and has supported long-term planning efforts. In 2023, the historic Dew Drop Inn was redeveloped to restore its original form as a hotel and music club, led by developer Curtis Doucette. An Art Place Grant was awarded to acquire land and renovate a historic building to become the MGIC's new headquarters. In the years since Small Center's involvement, the MGIC has acquired an additional building to expand its campus.

VISIONING

Terrytown Housing Plan

Strategic Redevelopment in a Historic Neighborhood, 2019

In recent years, Small Center has recognized a need for design and planning services beyond the Orleans Parish boundary. These projects extend the Center's work in the city to acknowledge the economic, social, and environmental connections with neighboring communities. As New Orleanians are faced with increased pressure to find affordable housing, many are moving to the surrounding cities and towns. Likewise, the impacts of climate change and land loss in Louisiana present shared planning challenges for communities within the region. Work with local and regional municipalities expands Small Center's ability to build dynamic coalitions and facilitate planning efforts to address regional challenges.

A suburb of New Orleans on the Westbank of the Mississippi River, Terrytown was the first planned development in Jefferson Parish, beginning in 1960 with fifteen model homes and marketed as low-cost to attract young families to the community. Cost savings came from the standardization of key elements, affordable land costs,

and modest house sizes. Common to the era, Terrytown's homes were designed in the style now known as "mid-century modern," which followed the International and Bauhaus movements and was widely adopted in America as post-WWII suburbs boomed. As in many inner-ring suburbs, Terrytown faced aging, and in some cases outdated, housing stock. This project represented an effort by the Parish, in partnership with residents, to address the challenges of preserving and revitalizing a historic neighborhood.

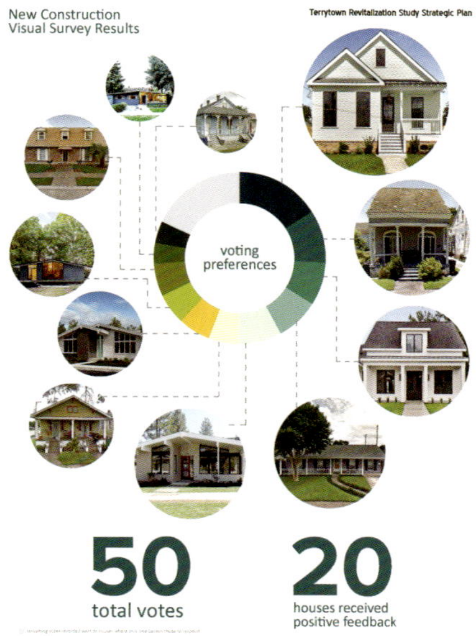

// ABOVE: Terrytown residents completed visual preference surveys to help define design guidelines for their neighborhood. //LEFT: Small Center led a series of community meetings with Terrytown residents and leaders from Jefferson Parish.

The Terrytown Housing Revitalization Strategic Plan brought together the Jefferson Parish Planning Department, Jefferson Parish Economic Development Commission (JEDCO), Terrytown Civic Association, and other partners to explore means of neighborhood revitalization through improvements to housing stock. The coalition ensured decision makers were at the table with residents and neighborhood leaders to offer a variety of perspectives as a strategic plan was developed. Building support across groups led to swift implementation.

Small Center worked with JEDCO and the Parish Planning Office to lead a series of five public engagement meetings throughout 2019, keeping Terrytown residents involved and updated as the process of crafting housing designs and regulatory incentives proceeded. Residents participated in a visual preference survey, interactive design discussions, online surveys, and one-on-one discussions about design options for housing and landscaping, including water management through green infrastructure. Small Center also engaged with the New Orleans Metropolitan Association of Realtors and the Home Builders Association of Greater New Orleans to better understand the motives behind recent sales and the costs associated with common renovations in the area.

The resulting strategic plan provides a suite of tools to improve the housing stock and neighborhood quality of life in Terrytown. Its intended audience was vast,

// ABOVE: Jefferson Parish constructed a model home to demonstrate their committment to the revitalization effort.

giving resources to residents, public officials, and supporting organizations. It also provided support to industries such as civic groups, banks, homebuilders, commercial developers, and businesses. Small Center's design guidelines provide free ideas for renovations and newly built homes appropriate to the historic, mid-century modern context of the neighborhood. The project came to fruition in 2020 with the building of one model home design, and in 2024 Jefferson Parish launched a façade renovation program that emerged from the planning effort.

Small Center often conducts planning projects. Early schematic designs inform municipal officials about the issues surrounding a given commercial corridor, downtown plan, sustainability plan, or other area of focus. Thanks to a committed municipal partner, this project provided an opportunity to move from engagement to implementation. In a region experiencing "planning fatigue" due to many rounds of disaster recovery planning that promised much and delivered little, projects that are quickly implemented and clearly incorporate public feedback give credence to future planning work and help to ensure wide public participation in such efforts. such efforts.

EXHIBIT

Extractivism

Telling the Story of Land Through Family, 2023

The exhibit *Extractivism* told the story of one Louisiana family against the backdrop of extractive economies, from slavery to petrochemical production. The project was part of a series of exhibits that aimed to create new partnerships and interdisciplinary dialogue between academics, nonprofits, and local artists. Each exhibit explored pressing issues around land and the built environment. Extractivism was facilitated, and shaped, by Small Center but curated by outside partners. In part, this incorporation of outside partners was done with the intent to center a diversity of voices from across New Orleans and the region. The Center's public programming has helped to shape coalitions around major issues, including affordable housing, cultural preservation, water management, activism, and criminal justice reform. Public programs can build attendees' advocacy skills and knowledge about New Orleans and the region. Focused coalitions and an engaged public are both critical in effecting lasting change.

For *Extractivism,* local writer Anya Groner and Memphis artist/documentarian Jazmin Miller took over Small Center's community storefront space to share an

impactful visual story, using photography, film, original reporting, and historical artifacts. For two years, Miller and Groner documented the history of Cancer Alley, an eighty-five-mile stretch of land along the Mississippi River between Baton Rouge and New Orleans which contains over 150 petrochemical plants and refineries. Their work grew out of Miller's research into her own family, which has owned land in Louisiana's St. James Parish for a century. The exhibit explored the challenges of Black descendant communities surviving and thriving in Cancer Alley. Land ownership with a sustained, rich connection to culture and family, the exhibit showed, is at risk from heavy industry, chemical plants, and the fight over the largest proposed plastics manufacturing facility in the country.

The exhibit featured clips from Miller's documentary film, *Jonesland,* telling the story of her family's history in this region–from chattel slavery to land ownership to the current onslaught of petrochemical refining and manufacturing. Atmospheric scenes from the film were paired with artifacts from the family's agricultural and rural life to bring visitors onto the land where the Jones family raised generations of children, even as their existence was regularly threatened. Groner's journalism documented the consequences of centuries of extraction along the Mississippi River. As a reporter-producer for the Monument Lab podcast *Plot of Land*, Miller chronicled the journey to uncover this family's history and uncertain future. Excerpts from the podcast, including on-site interviews, allowed exhibit visitors to listen to these stories while immersed in the artifacts and visual representations.

Facilitating and hosting exhibits like *Extractivism* continues to build Small Center's network of nonprofits and artists while spurring public knowledge and curiosity

about the built environment. All exhibitions are framed by issues of architecture or planning and contribute to discussions that center the role of the built environment in shaping everyday life. *Extractivism* explored inequity in planning and zoning processes, highlighting the need to amplify community voices.

// ABOVE + LEFT: Artifacts and film projections bring exhibition visitors into the world of Louisiana's river parishes.

Is This Architecture?

Jackson Blalock

The former member of Transitional Spaces, nonprofit steward of Parisite Skate Park, relays the regulatory hurdles and partnerships needed to achieve a first-of-its-kind skate park, and the ongoing effort to maintain it as an inclusive recreational space.

Phone calls bounced around New Orleans's skateboarding community: "The Peach O is gone!" Heavy machinery had just wiped away years of skateboarders' work in a matter of minutes. The Peach Orchard, New Orleans's most popular skate spot, was rubble.

Roll forward to 2013, when those same skater-builders applied lessons learned from the demolition; this time, they poured concrete on vacant, city-owned land below Interstate 610 at the intersection of Paris Avenue and Pleasure Street ("Paris site"). Under the highway, wheels smacked against new concrete transitions, music reverberated, and the popular refrain was, "The City of New Orleans will never destroy the only skatepark in town!"

When well-dressed city staff in dark sunglasses showed up to threaten demolition, we reached out to Tulane's Small Center. While they showed interest, there wasn't

a clear match-up. Former Director Maurice Cox visited Parisite, pondering aloud, "Is this architecture?" How could design students get relevant training when skaters were doing a fine job of designing and building this much-needed park themselves, outside the law?

Push onward to 2015, as skateboarders launched over the heads of beaming City of New Orleans' officials while Mayor Mitch Landrieu cut into a celebratory sixteen-foot-long sandwich. Parisite Skatepark's official opening and "Reuben-Cutting" hinted at a more skate-friendly city that could better represent local youth. Those of us on this roller coaster were overjoyed, yet scratched our heads: how did we get here?

One could point to hard work; skateboarders sweated and toiled at all hours, enduring concrete burns and sore backs while building Parisite's first ramps and founding the nonprofit "Transitional Spaces" to advance fundraising and partnerships. One could also point to overwhelming need: New Orleans was the largest U.S. city without a public skatepark, unable to serve the 25,000 skaters in the greater New Orleans area. Or perhaps it was the self-driven and stubborn do-it-yourself ethic embedded in "Parisite DIY Skatepark," riffing off of legendary DIY skateparks built elsewhere, often at odds with local regulations.

These factors and more merged to create Parisite, a space glued together by a network of supporters. Parisite's DIY ethic was coupled with a healthy recognition of our scrappy team's limitations, embracing others' involvement as long as their intentions were collaborative. Small Center pieced into Parisite's puzzle at a critical time in its evolution, when approaching legal enforcement could have squashed its celebratory experimentation. The Center answered questions like:

What could we do when the City threatened demolition of unpermitted ramps? Emilie Taylor Welty at Small Center connected us with an engineer who could advise us on structural revisions, stamp drawings, and show the City that they could accept the ramps' existence.

Where would funds come from? We weren't going to sell enough water bottles to fund this endeavor. Tulane assisted with grant proposals while contributing their own funds, technical expertise, and encouragement to move pieces of the park forward while ensuring skaters led the design.

How could we get faceless state and federal organizations' attention to approve of work under the interstate? Small Center staff leaned in with Tulane's heft to ensure Louisiana State Department of Transportation and the Federal Highway Administration came to the table, coaching Transitional Spaces' volunteers to steer these meetings to productive results.

How could we convince the City that Parisite was worthy of their time and support? Tulane's Doug Harmon sat alongside us through countless meetings, navigating red tape and skeptical city staff while showing decision-makers how Parisite was a big win for the City. Tulane students' design-build work beautified the park, reduced local flooding, and created an accessible public space, showing the City that this "skatepark problem" was actually a great asset.

Importantly, it's not just what Small Center did, but how they did it. The skater-builders didn't exhibit territorial ownership of Parisite but instead invited anyone to join and follow their own personal energy. Tulane's Small Center reflected this labor of love as they came to the skatepark with open ears. Their commitment to help was flexible, adapting to emerging needs in ways that expanded what architecture could be. They helped navigate labyrinthine bureaucracies, provided invaluable design and implementation assistance, supported emerging relationships across relevant audiences, and more. In doing so, they uncovered unexpected ways for designers and educators to humbly contribute to community-driven coalitions. Small Center helped strengthen and communicate Transitional Spaces' values throughout these processes–meeting community members where they were at–to build a park recognized nationally for its inclusive and innovative approach.

Skaters still manage Parisite as it continues to grow in organic ways that defy expectations. Small Center's fingerprints are all over Parisite, but you won't find anything resembling a building. *Is this architecture?*

Extractivism

Anya Groner & Jazmin Miller

Writer Anya Groner and Artist/Educator Jazmin Miller discuss the process of telling one family's story with the aim of shedding light on centuries of extraction from Black communities in rural Louisiana.

Three times in life have I felt the earth tremble.

The first time occurred nearly ten years ago on a Saturday morning. My bed rocked during a minor earthquake in Memphis, Tennessee. The second time was during the pandemic, not long after learning that my family's land (sixty-six acres we call "Jonesland") sits atop an oil reserve. While going through courthouse conveyances in St. James Parish, Louisiana, I discovered my great-great-great grandmother's sale-of-slave record, tied to a plantation only two lots away from my family's current land. My curiosity about my family's history, the elders' secrecy about the oil beneath their houses, and their fear of the outside world discovering Jonesland's natural resources converged, and the room moved beneath me. The third time I felt the earth move was on May 8, 2021, when I read Anya Groner's article titled "Louisiana Chemical Plants are Thriving Off Slavery" in *The Atlantic.*

My curiosity about St. James Parish started with a drive along River Road, the snaking rural highway that runs parallel to the Mississippi River levee. I was looking for someplace new to walk my dog when I found myself inside of a toxic dystopia. Pipes ran along one side of the road, stadium-sized holding tanks along the other. Flaming smokestacks towered above. I'd heard there were plantations out this way, but not industry, and certainly not industry of this scale. What was the relationship between the two? How did plantations become plants? And how do the people who live here, tucked between sugar cane fields and petrochemical plants, feel about their behemoth neighbors?

Not long after, I pitched a story about environmental advocate Sharon Lavigne and her fight to stop Formosa Plastics from building a $9.4 billion industrial megaplex a stone's throw from her house, her family's gravesites, and the local elementary school, to The Atlantic. *And that's how Jazzy found me. Her family owned 66 acres down the road from Sharon. She'd traced their lineage to a nearby plantation. She was making a documentary. Could I spare a few minutes to talk?*

"I am not a camera person. I'm a journalist. I hide behind paper..." Anya reiterated to me after I found a good angle and placed the microphone.

"I'm really not a behind-the-camera person," I responded. As it turns out, we began our friendship and collaboration telling stories in ways that were new to both of us.

Months later, I received a call. Anya was reporting for a podcast called *Plot of Land* and wanted to work with me on an episode about Louisiana's extractive economy. She didn't want to use my story. Instead, she wanted to uplift it by reporting on the documentary I was in the process of making. Was I interested?

Jazzy was so generous. In the dim light of Mount Calvary Baptist Church, she showed me maps, speculated about why so much of her family's history had been lost, and told me frankly what recovering those stories meant. Then, she introduced me to her people. Uncle LJ, Papa, and Aunt Laverne spoke to me from the plush red pews by the pulpit. I sampled fresh baked pie at Aunt Cora's house as she told me about unity, how in her family, "What one had, the other had, too." Another day, we strolled through Jonesland, from porch to garden to the animal pens where Wjanquil's pigs and chickens and hunting dogs stayed. I was finally starting to understand how much autonomy and joy and safety that land provided and why so many generations forwent oil wealth to keep those acres intact.

We finished the podcast and then Small Center put out a call for a residency that allowed local artists to collaboratively exhibit their work. Jazzy and I leapt. For three years, we'd worked in parallel. Now, I could put my writing and oral histories alongside her photography and film. Small Center worked with us to curate, display, and share a rich, interactive story. Then we welcomed in the public, creating dialogue around past challenges and current organizing efforts.

A documentary. A podcast. An exhibit. We stumbled into three collaborative mediums together, becoming colleagues, friends, and sisters in the process. Looking back on the process, I'll say this, Anya and I do three things really well. (1) We listen, which is far more important than having something to say. (2) We exercise flexibility. I cannot tell you how many times we have had to shift, adapt, and change directions. (3) We advocate for ourselves, for justice, for those exposed to the ills of petrochemical industries, and for forgotten history. Perhaps most importantly, we advocate for each other, seeing the potential in each other even when we struggle to see it in ourselves. We would have been alright to do this work alone, but in partnership, we've switched mediums, shared insights, introduced family members, offered critique, and most of all integrated generosity.

For centuries, extraction has ravished Louisiana's sugar parishes, destroying the environment and harming the people who live there. The damage is profound. And while it can't be undone, I like to think that, perhaps, in collaboration and community, we're taking a small step in the opposite direction. We're no longer taking from this place. In our one small way, we're putting pieces back together.

Understanding Power

Sarah Satterlee

The former Small Center Public Interest Design Fellow reflects on lessons of working with underserved communities reshaped her ideas of what architecture can do.

The first Tuesday of the first semester of my Masters of Architecture at Tulane, I found myself with a dozen classmates in an empty lot in a part of the city to which I had never been. Around the corner appeared several larger-than-life, headdress-wearing drummers showing off their beaded suits to welcome us to the neighborhood. They were members of the Guardians of the Flame, a Mardi Gras Indian tribe in the Upper Ninth Ward with whom we would be working on a design-build project with Small Center. As a brand-new architecture student, I was thrilled to have the opportunity to swing a hammer and build something interesting. But it soon became clear that we were also being invited into a larger, more important conversation about the relationship between space, culture, and power. Over the next ten weeks, and throughout the rest of my time with Small Center, what I thought would be an education on concrete, glass, and steel turned into an exploration of more critical questions: Who has the power to shape the built environment? What voices are being

heard, heeded, or ignored? Who has the agency to stay somewhere, and who is being pushed out–and what attributes of strong communities do we gain or lose in the process?

During our work with Guardians of the Flame, our team was faced with this question: *How can we use a physical space to secure control over cultural capital?* Like other tribes, the Guardians carried on the long New Orleans African American tradition of masquerading with spectacular costumes and vibrant rhythms and dance. Their songs and stories were important artifacts ingrained in New Orleans's collective cultural lore. But recently, the group has been facing increasing reuse of their material without consent or compensation. They feared losing control over the cultural capital created by their people over decades of investment and care. A physical building could create space to protect these assets and their ability to build on, and share, them on their own terms.

Over the course of the semester, we constructed the Guardians Institute, a bright orange and shiny galvalume structure that provided space for costume archives, beading workshops, and a performance stage that spilled out onto Independence Street. The modern metal building stands out in the neighborhood, taking cues from the showy suits it houses.

Later that year, I was able to explore another neighborhood through the Columbus Greenway project. In many ways, Columbus Street was just like any other street in the Seventh Ward. It suffered from crumbling pavement, poor drainage resulting in frequent flooding, and ubiquitous blighted and vacant lots. When our group of students was invited to explore interventions, it didn't take long for us to see that this six-block stretch also had many unique strengths. The roadway was flat and relatively smooth, and since it was situated between several established bike routes, it was already being used as a bike thoroughfare. There was an impromptu community garden and an orchard that had popped up on an empty corner lot. Most importantly, there were lively and invested neighbors, many of whom hung out regularly on the lot at the corner of Columbus and N. Roman. There was almost always a game of horseshoes being played or a grill full of wings being prepared. Even with the issues created by disinvestment, all of these informal activities had already been serving as powerful tools for placemaking. We found ourselves asking: *How can we recognize and celebrate the activity that already happens on Columbus, and make it an easier and safer place to continue that activity?*

//LEFT: Students and staff put the final touches on the Guardians Institute. Photo: Andrea Mabry

After several "design meetings" that involved dozens of shucked oysters, and after a couple of neighborhood build days, the neighborhood had a new shade structure with a long gathering table and stadium seating for horseshoe spectators. The construction of something permanent was a small act of claiming space for what had previously been informal and temporary. We also created a formal plan for needed infrastructure updates, in hopes that the city would recognize the neighborhood's assets and invest its own resources to build the Columbus Greenway into the lively, functional, beautiful corridor it had the potential to be.

Eleven years later, I'm still practicing community design, working with populations whose power to take up space is constantly challenged. Through my work at Community First Village, I lead the design and development of supportive housing communities for folks coming out of chronic homelessness. Most of our neighbors have a variety of disabilities, mental illnesses, and trauma stories that have contributed to years, or even decades, of social isolation. They've been pushed to the margins socially and spatially. In spite of this (and sometimes because of this), our neighbors are the most interesting, vibrant, weird, loving, no-bullshit people I've ever been around, and we've found that a community made up of these folks is imbued with the same powerful attributes. While many municipalities try to "solve" homelessness by simply providing shelter in a way that conveniently removes the unhoused from public view, we are trying to ask a different question that flips the narrative: *How do we create communities that don't just begrudgingly ration space for the marginalized, but instead see their uniqueness, strengths, and shared experience as the very foundation to build upon?*

In many ways, starting my career in New Orleans was the beginning of my exploration of these ideas. We have always built our lives around the delightful, the celebratory, the strength we find in adversity. We know what it's like to live life in a tenuous space, whether that's facing climate change or dealing with institutionalized obstacles. Similarly, Small Center ingrained in me a way to think and act as a designer who can entertain complex questions and better understand the power differentials that I am either enabling or undoing. My experiences there fostered the curiosity and humility required to act responsibly as an extension of the various populations we serve. I've never known architecture any other way.

//LEFT: Interior museum space displays Mardi Gras Indian suits and paraphernalia at the Guardians Institute. Photo: Andrea Mabry

6

Stewarding Small Steps Toward Big Changes

"Playbooks of the past will not meet future needs. We need to imagine, develop, and test new inclusive approaches to shaping the city."

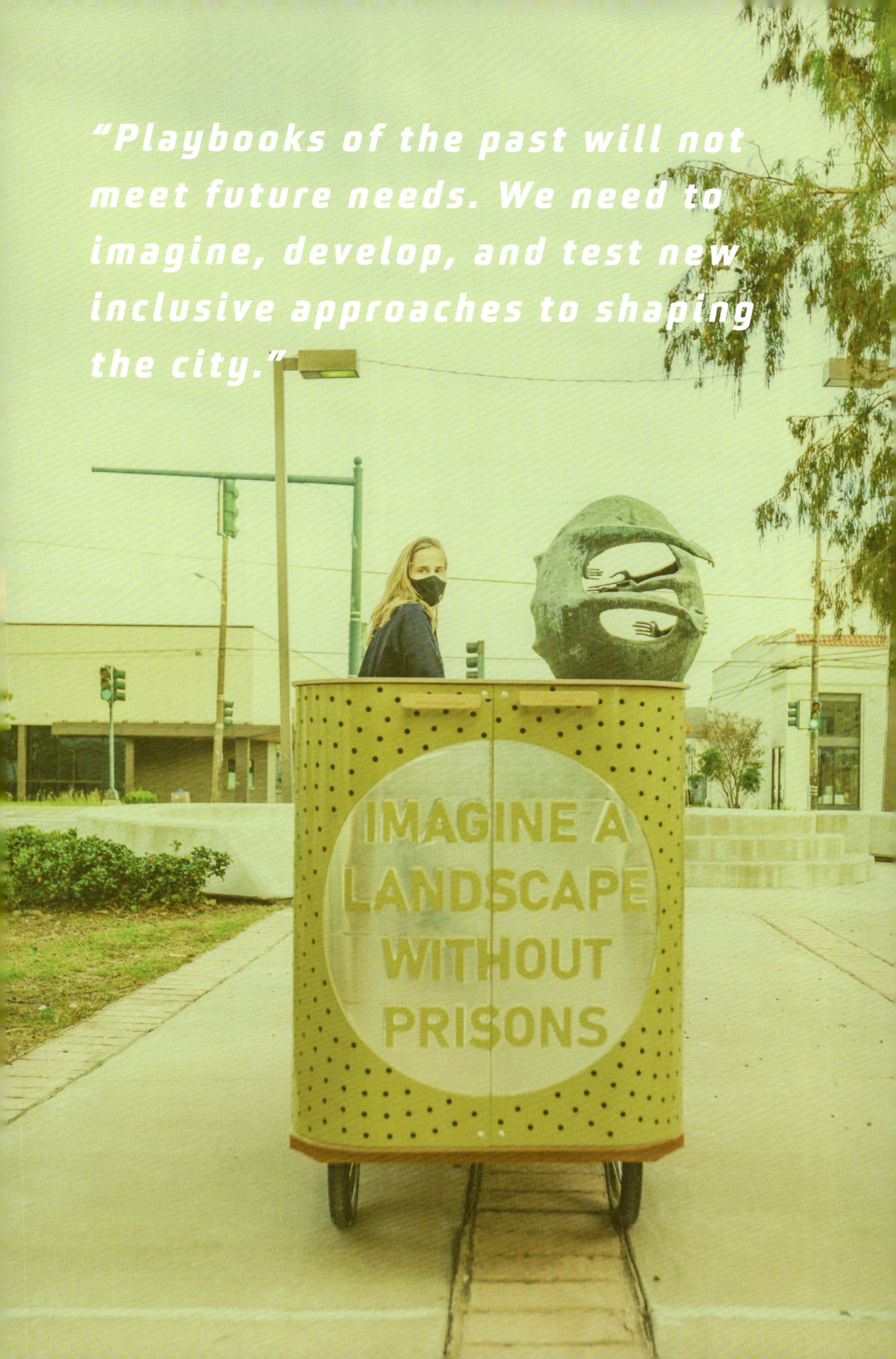

At Small Center's founding in 2005, in the wake of Hurricane Katrina, New Orleans's needs were immediate and urgent. The Center's early work responded to the urgency of this context, but its focus has since shifted to supporting long-term, systemic change. However, much of the systemic change needed is nonetheless related to climate emergencies. New Orleans, like other cities along the coastline, continues to grapple with complex environmental challenges twenty years since the hurricane. Every 100 minutes, it is estimated that Louisiana's coastline loses the equivalent of one football field of land. Coastal erosion increases the city's vulnerability to hurricane storm surges, compounding the potential impacts of more frequent and more intense Gulf Coast storms due to climate change. Residents, and those hoping to return to the city, continue to face pressures of housing affordability related to the climate emergency as insurers flee the state. These current concerns demonstrate that the playbooks of the past will not meet future needs. We need to imagine, develop, and test new approaches to shaping the city.

Architects bring technical expertise to these pressing issues, but this expertise cannot be used according to the flawed models of the past. It is important to look beyond design's traditional role–as a way to fix problems caused by old methods of city-making–and to reframe it as a way to contribute new ideas to larger movements for change. The Center accomplishes this by staying curious and open to the concerns of its collaborators, looking toward the transformation of oppressive systems rather than jumping to immediate solutions.

// ABOVE: Sprout's pavilion for their urban farm comes to life. Photo: Fernando Lopez-Sanchez

The Center carefully selects its collaborators to ensure that the projects it undertakes align with the systemic issues deemed most pressing by the community. Small Center prioritizes partnerships with organizations that serve marginalized groups and that have established themselves as trusted resources within the communities they serve. These organizations offer services that directly address the wellbeing and needs of their communities, often through collective and cooperative models that build community power. Small Center's early work, which prioritized small but visible outcomes, offered a counterpoint to the fruitless city planning meetings that took place around the time of its founding. As the Center has evolved, its work has become forward-looking, while still attending to the complexity and needs of the present.

Pursuing architectural services is an opportunity to look to the future. For some organizations, the future is framed by the need to claim permanent and visible space for their work. For others, it is about imagining a society so transformed that their work is no longer needed. Design offers an opportunity to balance the immediate, practical considerations of the present with broader agendas for social justice. Small Center's work aims to take this one step further by creating tangible models, whether in built or image form, for these alternative futures, making these possible realities visible. Visible ideas can more easily become part of the public's imagination of what is achievable. As described in previous chapters, graphic advocacy offers one means of visualizing possibilities and building coalitions. Physical prototypes can make these visions into reality, demonstrating inhabitable models that are tested, studied, refined, and replicable.

The Center's projects, which are community-designed, often house community-led programming, meaning that they are prototypes for an alternative, collaborative version of the city. In recent years, community engagement and participation have become increasingly accepted in architecture as the discipline grapples with its role in addressing equity and providing a public service. However, it is still uncomfortable territory for many architecture firms. Working deeply with community stakeholders takes time to build trust, to define a project's scope, to balance action with reflection, and to find funding. It is expensive and can disrupt established ways of working. Nevertheless, working methods that ensure everyone has a voice in imagining and shaping the future of their city are essential to architecture's relevance. Small Center equips students with skills to facilitate and join these discussions. Students bring the ethics and skills necessary to work in community, learned at the Center, into their future careers, whether in traditional architecture, allied fields, or testing new models elsewhere. Small Center's work, holding space for community solidarity, ensures that contemporary architecture responds to expressed needs and local context; this is what excellence in design means today.

Debates continue within schools of architecture and design about what counts as architectural scholarship and research. Small Center's work offers one model to answer this question. The Center conducts traditional research into design and materials, but tests ideas as site-specific, applied research. Through this process, the Center contributes to the current discourse about how architects can apply their skills to a broader range of social concerns and how architectural instruction can draw from participatory action research methods. The work can at once be beautiful, functional, and shaped by its cultural and environmental context. The Center's contribution to the city is itself a model of scholarly work: the product of integration and synthesis across knowledge domains and social connections. As discussed in previous chapters, Small Center positions design conversations as opportunities to build relationships and advocate for broader change together.

Designers can imagine built projects that create lasting physical changes to an environment. Architecture can also enshrine existing activities, like skateboarding or recurring games of horseshoes, formally marking and accepting them into the built environment. This protects place-based activities that would languish without formal sanctioning. These meaningful additions to the city's fabric preserve and create community spaces, allowing partner organizations to fulfill their missions. Small Center's work differs from other architecture practices because it partners with organizations whose missions extend beyond typical architectural scopes, filling gaps created by a history of disinvestment in communities of color and low-income neighborhoods. To transform society in the long-term requires more than mere physical interventions, and is instead built upon long-lasting collaborations within the community.

Though Small Center requires that partner organizations have site control of the property for which the Center will design a project, organizations are not guaranteed to stay in one place forever. Past projects, such as the Ozanam Inn Day Space, have been demolished as organizations have relocated to other sites, navigating neighborhood dynamics, tight budgets, and the need to remain accessible to the populations they serve. The demolition of a project is not an end, since part of the Center's design process involves building a relationship that survives the physical space. The work lives on in the dynamics that informed the design process, whether that entails continued consulting, issue advocacy, or connecting partners with additional resources.

Small Center supports groups already working for change by seeking alliances and partnerships that amplify existing efforts. Working in collaboration means bringing new perspectives to identify new ways of doing things. Over time, these creative, nimble solutions compound, as the number of diverse voices increases, solving complex and seemingly intractable problems.

Though the footprint of the Center's work is often small in scale, it contributes to organizations working toward big social transformations. The projects in this chapter demonstrate the importance of envisioning alternative futures with wild imagination and the opportunity for designers to help facilitate a reality in which all residents might flourish. A city with permanently affordable housing. A garden-based wellness hub in every neighborhood. A world without prisons. Through process and product, the Center aims to prototype the social dynamics and physical conditions of more just and sustainable futures.

---

[37] Brady R. Couvillion, Holly Beck, Donald Schoolmaster, and Michelle Fischer, *Land area Change in Coastal Louisiana (1932 to 2016): Scientific Investigations Map 3381* (U.S. Geological Survey, 2017), https://doi.org/10.3133/sim3381.

VISIONING

Jane Place Neighborhood Sustainability Initiative

Advocating for Collective Affordable Housing, 2011, 2016

Small Center worked with Jane Place Neighborhood Sustainability Initiative to envision a permanently affordable cooperative housing structure. Research into the frameworks of Community Land Trust models and the legal complexities of cooperative housing informed the development of the Jane Place prototype, which envisioned the renovation of a three-story, multi-family building. Though Small Center's architectural design was not realized, the research informed Jane Place's approach to building permanently affordable housing units in the heart of the city. Small Center's collaborative process brought together housing advocates, informed an exhibit on affordable housing, and set the stage for the organization to continue expanding its affordable property holdings.

// ABOVE: The design team sketches options for the warehouse renovation.
// OPPOSITE: A rendering depicts affordable housing above a community gathering center and back yard suitable for events.

Jane Place was created in response to an acute housing need in New Orleans. In the wake of Hurricane Katrina, housing costs rose dramatically and never returned to pre-storm levels, when New Orleans was widely recognized as an affordable place to live and housing costs more closely aligned with the city's low-wage hospitality and tourism jobs. The 2013 American Community Survey data showed that residents in the Jane Place target neighborhoods were majority renters, seventy-nine percent of whom were rent-burdened, paying more than thirty percent of their income on housing, and often much more. Jane Place began as a grassroots organization within Nowe Miasto, a collective living, performance, art, and community space that served as an organizing hub for local activists from 1999 to 2005. This converted warehouse space became an incubator, sustainer, and supporter of community-based projects that used the building for activities and events. It is often these kinds of organizations and collectives, operating as close to the ground as possible, that recognize, mobilize and respond to needs as they are being experienced in the community in real time.

Small Center worked with Tulane School of Architecture's nascent Master of Sustainable Real Estate Development program to scope and design housing options within Jane Place's two properties, working to understand legal complexities by researching cooperative housing in other cities, and providing research to help aid decision-making for the nonprofit's future. Small Center's team traveled to New York City to research precedents. Based on what the team found, they developed reports outlining the framework for a Community Land Trust and a vision for the Jane Place buildings. The team also did schematic design work for the housing units, providing floor plans, and interior and exterior renderings. Jane Place rehabilitated the building into four units of permanently affordable rental housing available to families with incomes at or below sixty percent of Area Median Income. The historic building is the first permanently affordable apartment building owned by a Community Land Trust in New Orleans.

Building a broad coalition to achieve a project often results in additional collaborations. Small Center built upon this work in the affordable housing arena by partnering with Home by Hand, another local nonprofit affordable housing developer. Home by Hand also used the Community Land Trust model with land acquired from the New Orleans Redevelopment Authority and has now produced over forty homes from around six initial prototypes developed for the project.

Working closely with a partner on one project can also lead to subsequent collaborative efforts, which was the case with Small Center and Jane Place. A second project contemplated the renovation of Jane Place's original warehouse building into a new headquarters and community meeting space, including additional affordable housing units. While this renovation project was not ultimately constructed, the yearlong collaboration allowed Jane Place to design alongside Small Center, analyze costs, and establish investment priorities as their organization continued to expand.

VISIONING

Vision House

Envisioning a New Home through Trauma-Informed Design, 2015 - 2016

Small Center collaborated with Women with a Vision (WWAV) to design "Vision House," a new headquarters for the organization. In the aftermath of an arson attack on its former location, WWAV worked with Small Center to redesign a building donated to the organization that would serve the needs of its clients and accommodate its growing staff.

WWAV does essential work for women in New Orleans, providing educational and job training services, court-sanctioned diversion programs keeping women out of jail, trauma care, and more. Small Center designed an engagement process sensitive to the needs of WWAV's diverse clientele. A small team of students, staff, and faculty studied trauma-informed design. Navigating the organization's safety protocols, the students created sensitive yet functional designs, including multiple

secure entrances designed to serve different client groups. The engagement process included engagement sessions with multiple constituencies to envision how the future, expanded needs of the organization might look.

The project team redesigned a traditional New Orleans "double shotgun" home to accommodate WWAV's staff, programming, and events. The product was a graphic document to be leveraged in the pursuit of project funding and development. Students and faculty closely considered the spatial needs of the expanding organization, building on its long-running success while better accommodating staff and expanded programming. Small Center's design team observed current operations, interviewed staff and clientele, and included all stakeholders in reviews of proposed designs. This engagement and on-site research allowed the team to learn how staff utilize space for programming. As a result, the design provided a careful mix of active service areas, quiet sanctuaries, private staff space, and outdoor respite. The collaborative effort packaged schematic designs, architectural plans, and budgets into one document to serve as a basis for project fundraising and as a roadmap for implementation. Small Center also hosted project work-sessions to explain the project and process to interested funders and potential promotional partners.

Despite a robust engagement and design process, WWAV did not renovate and move into the proposed building. Even as the collaborative design developed, the organization had to consider an expanding staff, speculative funding, and future programming that would mean it would soon outgrow the planned location. Despite this, there was inherent value in the engaged design process and the schematic architectural designs it produced, as they determined what was feasible and defined the needs of the organization. While, ultimately, the newly acquired building was mismatched with WWAV's growth, the process allowed the organization to quantify its spatial needs and begin budget prioritization towards their needed expansion. WWAV continues to provide critical services in New Orleans and now operates from a new headquarters just around the corner from Small Center in the Central City neighborhood.

// ABOVE: The design team surveys the gutted building and works with WWAV to create a redevelopment plan.
// OPPOSITE: WWAV shares information about their organization to aid the design team in understanding the multiple constituencies for the new headquarters.

BUILD

FARMacia

Building a Community Garden, 2019

Small Center worked with local nonprofit NewCorp to design the FARMacia Wellness Hub, a signature initiative of its Seventh Ward Revitalization Project. The Hub aimed to improve community health by providing a space for wellness-focused activities and educational programming. Small Center's clever design held space for community possibility; the design process focused on creating a structure that represented Phase One of a larger community garden master plan. With scarce and very competitive grant funding for community nonprofits, the phased design allowed the organization to grow slowly, paced to its own capacity for site development and maintenance. The structure itself provided shade for community members, but also importantly offered a prototype for a garden-based wellness hub. Equally a space for entrepreneurs and community health advocates, it also built on the history of the site, which once housed the city's first Black female doctor.

Small Center's Public Interest Design Fellows developed a master plan for the nearly 7,500 square foot site and built the community gathering structure during a hot, humid New Orleans summer. Based on the needs and priorities identified by

NewCorp and community stakeholders during design charrettes that Spring, the master plan also included a butterfly garden for children's play, a bioswale to manage stormwater, a storage structure for equipment and materials, and a greenhouse for protected growing. The completed community gathering and shade structure incorporated the unique neighborhood street grid pattern known as "The Cut" into the front façade. Wood and ropes on the side elevations created a visual gradient. Alluding to the public/private nature of a shotgun house, the design situated open space in the front and more private and intimate spaces in the back of the site.

The final pavilion design pays homage to the iconic form of the single shotgun house type and serves as a reminder that such lots once contained homes full of vibrant life and rich history—Dr. Thelma Coffey-Boutte, the first Black woman to practice medicine in New Orleans, once resided on the site, making the desire to transform it into a hub for community wellness even richer. As planned, the site has developed slowly in subsequent years, now featuring a greenhouse, planter beds, murals, and other community health features. The project stands in dialogue with Small Center's other urban agriculture projects, including Grow Dat, Sugar Roots, Hollygrove Market & Farms, and Sprout pavilion. Committed to tackling issues larger than one site can address, Small Center improves conditions on the ground one project at a time, towards exponential change.

BUILD

Apothecarts

Mobilizing Prison Abolition and Healing, 2020

Small Center's design-build studio worked with the Prisoner's Apothecary on "Apothecarts," a series of mobile herbal medicine carts that make justice visible and healing accessible across the City of New Orleans. Built structures, even when small and/or mobile, can serve as signposts for an organization's mission, boosting awareness and bringing a larger movement to the people. The Apothecarts were designed to be deployed to community festivals and neighborhood events across the city. The carts are filled with plant medicine from the Prisoner's Apothecary and are used to catalyze public conversations at the intersection of healthcare, social justice, public art, and prison abolition.

The Apothecarts were developed in partnership with frequent Small Center collaborator and artist jackie sumell, director of Solitary Gardens, a nonprofit that brings awareness to the effects of the carceral system. The issue is of particular relevance in Louisiana, which regularly incarcerates more of its population per capita than any other state. Solitary Gardens focuses on the conditions within

// ABOVE: The Small Center team and partner jackie sumell create mock-ups to test scale, materials, and feasibility of the design.
// OPPOSITE: The completed mobile carts are displayed publicly in a parklet along MLK Boulevard.

solitary confinement. Of the 2.2 million incarcerated people in the United States, 80,000 to 100,000 are subjected to indefinite solitary confinement every day, with prisoners isolated for a minimum of twenty-three hours per day in a six-by-nine-foot (or smaller) concrete and steel cell. Architecture students were able to grapple with this spatial condition by helping to construct a "solitary garden," designed in the shape and layout of a typical cell. The team combined its research, engagement, and prototyping to create a unique and highly visible built project capable of bringing attention to the organization's mission and programming.

The Prisoner's Apothecary transforms plants grown in the Solitary Gardens into medicine for communities most deeply impacted by mass incarceration. The apothecary produces natural medicine, tea, tinctures, steams, and salves. The medicine is developed by people who are incarcerated and distributed to affected communities, giving those who are incarcerated a unique opportunity to heal the communities they are often accused of harming. Mobile carts, or "Apothecarts," were envisioned as a way to mobilize and distribute the apothecary's wares while educating the public on the issue of mass incarceration. Given this charge, Small Center students and faculty learned the uses, sites, and networks within which the carts would operate. The

team investigated a range of cart scales, functions, mechanical details, and materials. The final build resulted in two bike-pulled carts that are lightweight, strong, and transformable, designed to survive New Orleans's infamous street conditions and open to create welcoming spaces for conversation around healing, justice, and abolition.

The scale of the project—somewhat smaller than the Center's typical design-build—was selected in part to suit constraints dictated by the Covid-19 pandemic safety protocols. Working in small, safely distanced teams, students also took on a series of affiliated design projects: a schematic design proposal for the expansion of the Prisoner's Apothecary into a cafe, and graphic informational pocket guides to be distributed from the Apothecarts. The completed mobile carts are now housed at different locations, and have also been exhibited at MoMA PS1, the Ford Foundation, and San Jose Museum of Art.

The Apothecarts have won several national and international design awards, showing how an engaged design process and high-quality design outcomes can further an organization's message. They have been exhibited widely, serving equally well as an educational tool in these settings as when deployed in the field. Exhibitions at Small Center have often provided this type of loudspeaker for prevailing issues in New Orleans and for the work of its partner organizations. The *Play It Louder* exhibition below built directly on the Apothecarts project, bringing together architects, artists, and activists to spark community conversations.

EXHIBIT

Play It Louder

Exploring the Architecture of Carcerality, 2023

Funded by a grant from the National Endowment for the Arts, Small Center created an exhibition focused on sharing data about the carceral state to educate, illuminate, and engage, assembling creative voices across disciplines.

Too often, data dehumanizes, is incomprehensible, and can be used to manipulate the truth. Data about prisoners and the carceral state are sometimes unavailable or unreliable. *Play It Louder* was staged to counter these realities, creating space to collaboratively explore the architectures of carcerality alongside environmentally sustainable material research in pursuit of a more just future. Through design investigations, interactive artworks, and installations grounded in data and research, the exhibit aimed to reveal the impacts of carceral systems and provide a platform to explore alternatives.

Play It Louder was structured around physical objects, but aimed to use these artworks to close the gap between numbers and narratives along with an invitation

to engage, empathize, and reflect. The exhibit built on past partnerships with jackie sumell of Solitary Gardens and the John Thompson Legacy Center, which provided visual representations of the crippling red tape that can prevent even obvious cases of wrongful conviction from being adjudicated within a humane timeframe. The exhibit also featured artwork by RENEE ROYALE which incorporated site-specific materials and photography from prison sites across Louisiana, bringing the often remote and unseen issue to direct attention. Artist Langston Allston created a moving mural across the length of Small Center's storefront façade, featuring key statistics to explain the impact of the carceral state, and enticing new visitors to the exhibit. Students and faculty contributed research into the architectural and spatial aspects of the carceral state from prison design to surveillance. Students envisioned new material futures and constructed public gathering spaces that drew from the work of local abolitionists.

Small Center is uniquely positioned to amplify multiple views and voices on contentious issues. Operating at the intersection of many neighborhood groups and nonprofits, while based in academia, the Center can place research in dialogue with evocative artistic practice. It can highlight the work of partner organizations while exploring and explaining the spatial and architectural aspects of a given issue. The Center's work demonstrates creative making and design research as a critical form

// ABOVE: Layered works by artist RENEE ROYALE.
// OPPOSITE: An interactive feature revealed statistics about incarceration in Louisiana with the application of powdered charcoal by hand.

of scholarly practice. Exhibitions and public programming provide an opportunity for students to create and design in dialogue with local artists and practitioners. Small Center's accessible venue is a natural location to provide an ongoing discourse through artistic practice, research, and design.

Collaboration is Everything

jackie sumell

The Solitary Gardens Director reflects on the role of collaboration and creative practice in abolitionist work.

Solitary Gardens utilizes the principles of prison abolition, permaculture, and community power to facilitate unexpected exchanges between incarcerated people in solitary confinement and volunteers on the "outside." Each six-by-nine foot garden bed replicates the blueprint of a standard U.S. solitary confinement cell. The beds are designed and remotely "gardened" by incarcerated collaborators, known as "Solitary Gardeners." Through growing almanacs, written and photographic exchanges, and occasional prison visits, we translate the imaginations of incarcerated individuals into the ground by cultivating the plants that they choose. In this way, Solitary Gardens become portraits of those condemned deepest within our carceral system.

As prisons are the descendants of slavery, the garden beds are constructed from the ancestral byproducts of sugarcane, cotton, and tobacco, exposing the illusion that slavery was abolished in the U.S. These former chattel slave crops are grown

on-site in New Orleans, milled down, mixed with a special non-hydraulic lime, and then, through a rammed-earth process, sculpted into a form to produce the walls and components of the prison-cell-turned-garden-bed. I developed this process in 2015, calling it Revolutionary Mortar. When building Solitary Gardens, we aim to transform what were America's most lucrative chattel cash crops into a holistic outcome. The process allows us to reconcile our violent past with its effects on the present and to collectively construct a very different future. The Solitary Gardens both directly and metaphorically ask us to imagine a landscape without prisons. As the gardens mature, the architecture is overpowered by plant life, proving that nature—like hope, love, and imagination—will ultimately triumph over the harm humans impose on ourselves and on the planet.

As I have furthered this work, it has become increasingly apparent that the natural world, which has transcended all natural and human-made disasters, holds the answers. Within the ethos and existence of nature lies a blueprint for how we can transcend the madness that we humans have created, coerced, and forced into existence. I often say that the first, and possibly most critical, step to becoming an "abolitionist" is wonder. We must activate our curiosity to first understand why we have accepted social contracts and constructs that rely on punishment as the only response to harm, and then to explore alternatives.

I have fallen in love a thousand times in the garden. It serves as a wonderful training ground for the practice of wonder and, by extension, for abolition. I truly believe that all the social crises that we humans have created can be resolved by working with consent, curiosity, and in relationship to the natural world. I have learned this explicitly from a man who spent forty-one years in a six-by-nine foot cage, surrounded by concrete and steel, yet found his dignity, hope, and possibility in nature.

> I have tried many times to grow flowers and other seasonal plants here in this cell and it just won't work! The concrete and steel and particularly the small closed-in area stifles the growth of plant life and causes the plant to die long before it develops. -Herman Wallace, excerpt from a letter sent with paper flowers to jackie sumell, 2006

Let's consider prison abolition as a creative practice, and charge artists with the task of illustrating the impossible. This is our superpower and, as such, responsibility. Artists, creatives, visionaries—we are the feelers of society. We act as barometers, interpreters, emotional pressure gauges, and often as mystics. The job of the artist transcends the immediate, the madness, and the horror that society has created. And please remember, the artist is not only an artist, but also a citizen.

I believe the antidote to hopelessness is action. This is why oppressors seek to stamp out the imagination, the ideas behind change and movement. This collective, collaborative, sometimes messy work refuses to accept that. It demands that we collectively look into the systems with which we are complicit, in order to shift cultural and systemic responses to harm. We are combatting a powerful, dominant narrative of fear birthed out of racial capitalism. Creative practices are inherent to mapping solutions, sharing information, and inspiring radical change. Art should remind us to dream beyond what is deemed to be moral or just by the dominant culture. A large part of my practice is animated by a personal philosophy that we artists contend with the battleground of public memory and, as such, we have a social responsibility to repair the imagination. I am based in New Orleans, Louisiana, the incarceration capital of the world, where I not only continue the very important work of Herman's House, Solitary Gardens, The Abolitionist's Apothecary, The Abolitionist's Sanctuary, Growing Abolition, and several other advocacy-based, collaborative projects, but do so in deep relationship with currently and formerly incarcerated people. It is the only way I believe we can advance a radically imaginative, abolitionist vision fundamental to the blueprint for a community of care, a world without prisons, and the expansiveness of social practice.

I hope this work challenges us to remember a relationship with both nature and humanity that does not require retribution as the only explanation of justice. It should inspire us to imagine a landscape that exists without prisons. In a society whose imagination is crippled by personal and collective trauma, it is important–nay it is critical–to illustrate not only what is wrong with systems of injustice, but also what is possible.

While my projects may seem monumental, and often span decades, I always start small. Micro: a letter, a meal, a moment, a seed. And much like the natural world, I allow it to grow from there. This work can only be watered through relationships; otherwise, it becomes colonial, manufactured through the accepted pedagogy of white supremacy, racial capitalism, and cis-heteronormativity.

Change is the only constant. It is not only possible but a principle of abolition. We have to believe in the possibility of change to create systems that are antithetical to permanence. Systems that do not condemn in perpetuity but instead nurture, nourish and facilitate change. The current criminal punishment system relies on the rigidity of permanence: you are condemned to the worst mistake of your life, reduced to an existence as a number, and placed in the immutable confines of concrete and steel. My version of justice remembers that we, as a species and as individuals, are ever changing. If we invest in the potential of a person, rather than the harm they may or may not have caused, if we invest in change, we will create a new system that makes the existing system obsolete. Collaboration is everything, and it is ever ongoing. It's so funny to me when (artists) sign a piece of work and are like "look what I did." For fuck's sake, we are ALWAYS in collaboration. The walk we took that morning, the coffee we drank, the way the bird songs woke us, the temperature of the air, the arguments we got in with our human partners, or the way our doggos push our elbows just so and changes the marks on paper–all of it is collaboration, formal or informal.

I understand this is cultural, but I think it's both absurd and dangerous to believe you can, or should, do anything alone. The natural world not only transcends but alchemizes the hubris of human existence. Once we learn to honor that relationship, we can start to build relationships within our species. And I have come to witness that humans are complex, but when we get it together–fuck–we are amazing.

// ABOVE: Play It Louder exhibit, examining carceral conditions in Louisiana
// PREVIOUS (p234): The apothecarts on interactive display in City Park

Nourishing Change

Rashida Ferdinand

The Sankofa Community Development Corporation Executive Director discusses development of a mobile market to combat food deserts and the importance of partnership for working toward long-term change.

In 2013, Sankofa CDC launched its Mobile "Fresh Stop" Market, a collaboration between community-based organizations, health centers, schools, and faith-based groups. The permanent produce stand structure was established by retrofitting a truck to provide fresh produce to local residents. To develop the Mobile "Fresh Stop" Market, we worked with the Tulane Small Center and architectural students on various design possibilities for the retrofitted truck. The students developed concepts, engaged with community members who would benefit from the market, built mock-ups, and created the final mobile, pop-up produce stand structure that brought fresh food to our community.

// ABOVE & OPPOSITE: The mobile market folded out from the bed of a truck to create a dynamic interactive display of produce. Photos courtesy Sankofa CDC

Since the aftermath of the 2005 Hurricane Katrina disaster, the Lower Ninth Ward community experienced a severe lack of healthy and affordable food options. Fresh produce was not commonly available. There were no full-service grocery stores and corner stores predominantly sell ultra processed food products high in salt and sugar, contributing to disproportionate rates of diet-related health issues residents.

A key initiative of our efforts was the comprehensive healthy food-oriented development, which aimed to address food insecurity and contribute to neighborhood revitalization. The Mobile Market traveled throughout the Greater New Orleans Area to deliver fresh produce, reaching four neighborhoods throughout each week. It helped to raise awareness about the benefits of fresh produce consumption and the risks associated with diet-related diseases. We sourced produce from local farmers, food distributors, and the Sankofa Community Garden.

The outreach component of the Mobile Market helped foster a deeper connection with the community and allowed people to learn more about this initiative. We collaborated with various local organizations, including senior centers and early childhood centers, where parents could shop for fresh produce while picking up their children. The resilience of the Lower Ninth Ward community and extensive

// ABOVE: Local shoppers select produce from the mobile market. Photos courtesy Sankofa CDC

history of social justice remain as crucial assets to our work, with our commitment to socio-economic and health equity for our community. We are collectively working towards a healthier, more sustainable future.

Some of the key organizations that supported the Mobile Market initiative included Daughters of Charity Health Center at St. Cecilia's, a local clinic serving the Lower Ninth Ward, with a focus on low-income populations; City of New Orleans Health Department, providing nutrition education resources for Women, Infants, and Children (WIC) benefit recipients at the Sanchez Community Center; Healthy Start, offering prenatal nutrition education and community engagement for expecting mothers; Indian Springs Farmers' Cooperative Association, a cooperative of African American farmers from southern Mississippi that supplies fresh produce to the markets; Second Harvest Food Bank, a nonprofit that supports cooking and shopping education programs to help families make healthier food choices; Veterans Administration Medical Center, a key partner in connecting veterans to the Mobile Fresh Stop Market and the Vegetable Incentive Program; Xavier University Health and Wellness Center, collaborating on training community members about food justice and health inequity issues; A Community Voice, advocating for social justice and political empowerment in the Lower Ninth Ward; and Lower Ninth Ward Senior Citizens Center, serving as a community engagement hub for education and training.

Reimagining the Healer's Yard

Pam Broom

The local nonprofit leader and frequent Small Center collaborator shares the process of transforming vacant lots, adding built and landscape elements over time to achieve an active community health and wellness hub, FARMacia.

For twenty-seven years, I have been inspired by the transformative power of community-building, a concept I first encountered as an undergraduate at Tulane University. During a study abroad program in Barbados. I collaborated with the Gender Studies Unit at the University of the West Indies (UWI), Cave Hill, on a quality-of-life survey for a nearby village. Observing UWI students conduct the survey reinforced the importance of participatory, community-led engagement—an ethos that continues to guide my work.

In February 2017, I began consulting with NewCorp, Inc., a twenty-five-year-old, Black, female-led Community Development Financial Institution (CDFI) in New Orleans. Tasked with integrating urban agriculture and green infrastructure into their Seventh Ward Revitalization Project (7WRP), I worked to address systemic challenges through place-based strategies. This comprehensive initiative

// ABOVE: Rope and wood used to enclose the Farmacia pavilion create shade and playful shadows

sought to revitalize the community through arts, culture, economic development, health, workforce development, and sustainable housing. I leveraged garden-fresh food cultivation and water management as tools for neighborhood revitalization while addressing the critical need for authentic community involvement. Effective development begins with listening to the people being served.

Out of this collaborative process, the FARMacia Wellness Hub was born. Designed as a green space to cultivate food and medicinal plants, the FARMacia promotes wellness and equity within Black, Indigenous, and People of Color (BIPOC) communities. Its name merges "farm" with the Latinate "farmacia" (pharmacy), reflecting its mission to connect agriculture with health. Located at 1831-35 Old Roman Street, in the heart of the Seventh Ward's "The Cut," an irregular wedge in the otherwise regular street grid, the 7,500-square-foot site reimagines the land's legacy. Formerly home to Dr. Thelma Coffey-Boutte, New Orleans's first Black female physician, the FARMacia honors her history while fostering new opportunities for health and healing.

Community engagement has been central to the FARMacia's evolution. A pivotal moment occurred during a neighborhood association meeting when a resident shared that he grew up on the property, which his father had purchased from Dr. Coffey-Boutte. This history underscored the importance of connecting the project to local narratives. Inspired by the concept of "Reimagining the Healer's Yard," the

FARMacia strives to promote wellness as a civil and human right, rooted in the lived experiences of the community.

In 2019, Small Center partnered with NewCorp on a summer design-build initiative to bring this vision to life. Faculty members Jose Cotto and Emilie Taylor Welty facilitated a design charrette with residents, yielding plans for a Community Gathering House. This open-air structure, inspired by the traditional shotgun house, incorporates local history in its design. A steel grid on the façade maps the shape of "The Cut," symbolizing the connection between place and design.

Today, the FARMacia Wellness Hub stands as a testament to the power of urban agriculture as a catalyst for community transformation, health equity, and cultural preservation. Aligned with NewCorp's mission to foster community building through capital investment in small businesses and underserved entrepreneurs, the FARMacia is emerging as a hub of "green incubation." This innovative space supports "agripreneurs"–food and farm-related microenterprise operators–by providing opportunities to develop fresh, marketable food products while receiving comprehensive training in farming business skills. Regular healthy lifestyle activities hosted collaboratively with community-based partners ensure that the FARMacia reflects the voices and aspirations of the Seventh Ward community. A neighborhood member's description of the site as "sacred space" underscores its deeper significance, rooted in collective healing, resilience, and economic empowerment.

// BELOW: An early rendering envisions multiple shade pavilions.

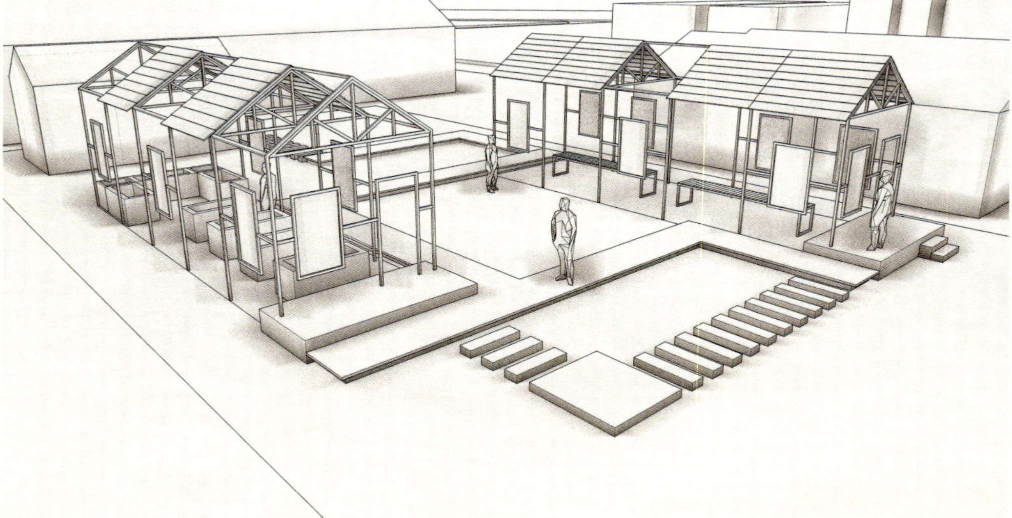

Afterword

To make something new in the world is an optimistic act. Whether that something is a small mobile food cart or a large urban skatepark, you are creating a new future on some small plot of land. And how that process unfolds, and the decisions made along the way, are all political, ethical, and social quandaries that move us closer to, or farther from, a just world.

Designing and building a project allows partners and neighbors to see immediate results—a shaded place to gather, a quiet room to work, a safe place to play, a physical affirmation of this moment and of each other. For architecture students, it offers a unique way of learning, a chance to wrestle with the space between idea and reality. Students must contend with materials, clients, budgets, gravity, technology, and each other as they realize a project on a one-to-one scale with real consequences. This radical form of education expands the classroom out into the world, exposing students to the physical implications of what they draw and requires them to engage with topics of ethical research and social responsibility. For partners, neighbors, and students, each project becomes a barn-raising: a moment of shared purpose and collective imagining made real. This process creates projects that create or affirm community, spaces that people love and are willing to fight to protect.

Small Center's combination of design education, direct action, and grassroots activism is informed by international efforts to democratize design. The Center's working methods are rooted in New Orleans' long history of social practice, which recognizes that environmental and social challenges are intertwined and that a just world is created by neighbors caring for one another. Across twenty years, the Center's leadership has changed, and so has the city. The work is adjusted to meet the needs and context of the time, but the guiding beliefs remain the same: to make the city better, the work must be collective and creative, and the time to act is now.

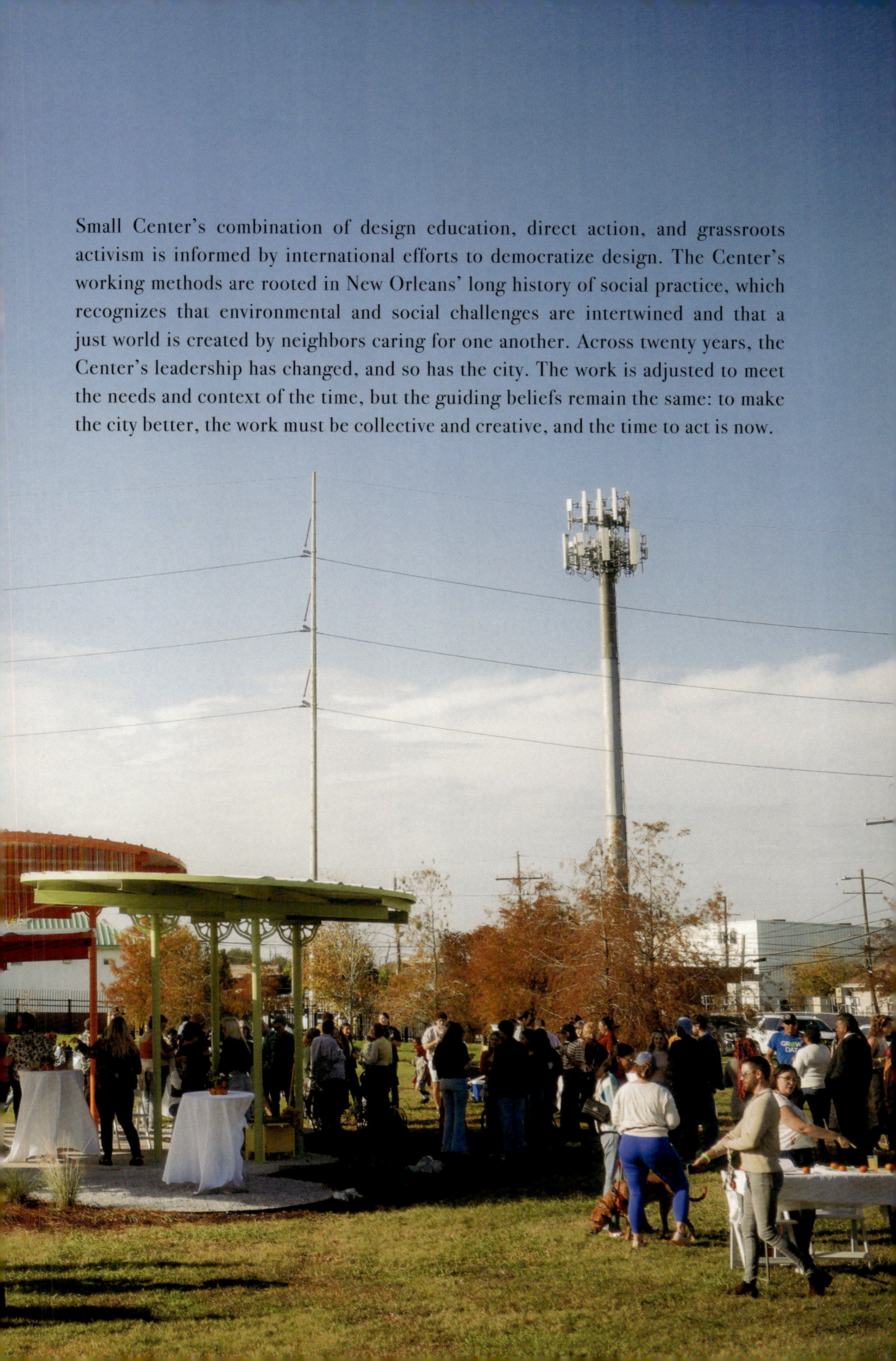

Chronology of Projects

A comprehensive list of project descriptions and collaborators is at small.tulane.edu. Projects are listed here by Title, Year, and Primary Project Partner(s), followed by an address for built works.

Holy Ghost House Design, 2005, with Neighborhood Housing Services of New Orleans, Inc.

Reinhabiting NOLA Conference, November 2005, with Xavier University, Tulane/Xavier Center for Bioenvironmental Research, and Loyola University

CITYbuild Consortium of Schools, 2006, with thirty national and international design-based programs, sixty faculty and more than 600 students, in partnership with twenty local community-based organizations, resulting in approximately sixteen structures and more than 200 proposals.

Adjudicated Properties Research, 2006, with Fannie Mae Foundation

CITYbuild: House of Dance and Feathers Museum, 2006, with Ronald Lewis, Kansas State University, and Project Locus • 1317 Tupelo Street

GREENbuild House, 2006, with Neighborhood Housing Services • 1939 Seventh Street

URBANbuild Prototype 1, 2006, with Neighborhood Housing Services • 1930 Dumaine Street

URBANbuild Prototype 2, 2007, with Neighborhood Housing Services • 2856 Dryades Street

Viet Village Urban Farm Visioning, 2006, with Mary Queen of Vietnam CDC and Louisiana State University Robert Reich School of Landscape Architecture

Idea Village Entrepreneur Center Visioning, 2006-2009, with Idea Village

URBANbuild Prototype 3, 2007, with Neighborhood Housing Services • 1900 Seventh Street

Skatepark Visioning, 2007, with New Orleans City Park

Salvage Focus the Nation Exhibit, 2008, with Rose Architectural Fellowship

Cornerstones Website and Publication, 2008, with Neighborhood Story Project

Hollygrove Market and Farm, 2008, with Carrollton-Hollygrove CDC, Trinity Christian Community, Louisiana State University Robert Reich School of Landscape Architecture, New Orleans Food & Farm Network • 8301 Olive Street (Demolished 2018)

Neighborhood Housing Services Design Build Center Visioning, 2008, with Neighborhood Housing Services

St Roch Project Housing Study, 2008, with Faubourg St Roch Project

How High?: Thoughts About Elevating Your House Publication, 2008-2009, with Louisiana State University Agriculture Center and University of New Orleans Center for Hazards Assessment, Response & Technology

Road Home Success Stories Advocacy, 2008, with Louisiana State University Agriculture Center

Deconfusing Green Event, 2008, with Neighborhood Housing Services

Tulane City Center Street Front Gallery Exhibition, 2008, with Tulane/Xavier Center for Bioenvironmental Research

T.R.E.E. Facility Upgrade Visioning, 2008, with T.R.E.E.

City Park Skate Park Visioning, 2008, City Park of New Orleans, Humidity Skateboards, Big Easy Roller Girls

URBANbuild Prototype 4, 2008, with Neighborhood Housing Services • 2036 Seventh Street

URBANbuild Open House, 2008, with Neighborhood Housing Services

Eco-Pavilion Sustainability Installation, 2008, with New Orleans City Park • in City Park Botanical Gardens (demolished)

Storypod Interview Studio and Workspace, 2009, with the Neighborhood Story Project

Circle Food Store Advocacy, 2009, with Circle Food Store

Backstreet Cultural Museum Exhibition and Performance Space, 2009, with Backstreet Cultural Museum • 116 Saint Claude Avenue

Hope Haven Campus Visioning, 2009, with Catholic Charities Archdiocese of New Orleans

Community Health Center Visioning, 2009, with Mary Queen of Viet Nam CDC

Green Crawl Event, 2009, with Louisiana State University Agriculture Center and Road Home

Hollygrove Growers Pavilion, 2009, with Carrollton-Hollygrove CDC and New Orleans Food &Farm Network • 8301 Olive Street (Demolished 2018)

Hollygrove Shade Units, 2009, with Carrollton-Hollygrove CDC and New Orleans Food & Farm Network • 8301 Olive Street (Demolished 2018)

Mid-City Community Garden Visioning, 2009, with Mid-City Community Garden

Hope Haven Farm and Cafe Hope Visioning, 2009, with Catholic Charities Archdiocese New Orleans

Streetcar Shelter Visioning, 2009-2010, with The New Orleans Regional Transportation Authority

Hollygrove Greenline Visioning, 2011 - 2015, with American Association of Retired Persons (AARP), Carrollton-Hollygrove CDC, DesignCorps, Engineers without Borders, Hollygrove Market & Farm, The New Orleans Food & Farm Network, and Trinity Christian Community

Covenant Farm Visioning, 2009, with The New Orleans Food & Farm Network and Covenant House New Orleans

Priestly School Outreach Lecture Series and Competition, 2008, with Priestley Charter School of Architecture and Construction

Modular Classroom Visioning, 2009, with Morgan Building Systems and Priestly School of Architecture & Construction

Green House Manual Publication, 2010

Scale Shift Urban Development Research, 2010

Allison Montana Institute of Art, Culture and Tradition Visioning, 2010, with Neighborhood Story Project

Project Sprout Land Management Visioning, 2009, with New Orleans Food & Farm Network and New Orleans Redevelopment Authority

All Souls Altar, 2010, with All Souls Episcopal Church, Episcopal Dioceses of Louisiana • 5500 St. Claude Avenue

Grow Dat Youth Farm, 2009-2011, with Grow Dat Youth Farm and City Park New Orleans • 150 Zachary Taylor Drive

The Green at Columbia Parc Visioning, 2010, with New Orleans Food & Farm Network and Bayou District Foundation

Hagars House Project Ish Outdoor Enrichment Room, 2010, with First Grace Community Alliance • Private Location

AL Davis Park Revitalization Visioning, 2010, with Harmony Oaks Neighborhood Association, New Orleans Neighborhood Development Collaborative, and Urban Strategies Inc.

Open Classroom Visioning, 2010, with Tulane University Campus Planning

Delassize Garden Structure, 2011, with Jericho Road Episcopal Housing Initiative, Friends of Faubourg Delassize, and New Orleans Food and Farm Network • 2912 Dryades Street

Urban Farming Toolkit Publication, 2011, with New Orleans Food and Farm Network

New Orleans Dance Collective Studio Visioning, 2011, with New Orleans Dance Collective

Jane Place 2739 Palmyra Affordable Housing Visioning, 2011, with Jane Place Neighborhood Sustainability Initiative

Hollygrove Greenline Shade Water Pavilion Design, 2014 - 2016, with Dana Brown & Associates and Trinity Christian Community

Guardians Institute Donald Harrison Sr. Museum and Legacy Performance Pavilion, 2011-2012, with Guardians Institute and Alembic Community Development • 1930 Independence Street

The Green Project Headquarters Visioning, 2012, with The Green Project

Columbus Greenway Initiative, 2014, with Neighborhood Story Project, Kids Walk Coalition, and New Orleans Food and Farm Network • Columbus Street, Lakeside of Claiborne

Playground Improvements Visioning, 2014, with Lusher Charter Elementary School

Candlelight Lounge Publication, 2011, with Cornerstones & Neighborhood Story Project

Morris Jeff Schoolyard Advocacy, 2011, with Morris Jeff Community School

Vacant Land Management Strategies Visioning, 2012, with Jericho Road Episcopal Housing Initiative

Pyramid Resources Wellness Institute Outdoor Space, 2012, with Pyramid Resources Wellness Institute • 3330 Canal Street

One in Six Mental Health Graphic Advocacy, 2012, with Pyramid Resources Wellness Institute

Lower Ninth Ward Food Action Plan, 2012-2014, with Center for Sustainable Engagement & Development

New Orleans Mission Expansion Visioning, 2013, with New Orleans Mission

Parisite Skatepark Visioning and Entry Plaza, 2013-2015, with Transitional Spaces • Paris Avenue under the I-610 Overpass

Magellan Street Garden, 2013, with Parkway Partners • 3320 Magellan Street, Algiers

Bayou Road Initiative Advocacy, 2013, with Broad Community Connections

Hung Dao Heritage Gardens Visioning, 2013 - 2014, with Hung Dao CDC

L9 Vision Coalition Advocacy, 2013-2014, with A Community Voice, Art House on the Levee, Holy Cross Neighborhood Association, Junebug Productions, L9 Center for the Arts, L9 Homeowners Association, Lower 9th Ward Village, Spackman Mossop & Michaels, and Tekrema Center for Art & Culture

Hollygrove Greenline Rain Gardens, 2013, with Carrollton-Hollygrove CDC, Dana Brown & Associates, and Trinity Christian Community • Multiple Residential Locations

Bastion Community of Resilience Charrettes, 2013, with Bastion Community of Resilience

LOOP NOLA Pavilion, 2014, with New Orleans City Park • 1031 Harrison Avenue

Project Home by Hand Visioning, 2014, with Project Home Again

St Claude Main Street Pocket Park Design, 2013-2014, with St. Claude Main Street, Project Homecoming

German School House Redevelopment Visioning, 2013, with US Heritage Powersports and Gulf Coast Housing Partnership

Façade RENEW Visioning and Design, 2013 – 2016, with New Orleans Redevelopment Authority and Clio Associates

Dew Drop Inn Visioning, 2013-2015, with the Painia Family, Milne Inspiration Center, and Harmony Neighborhood Development

Baronne Street Headquarters Furnishings, 2014 • 1725 Baronne Street

LaSalle Corridor: Mardi Gras Indians Cultural Corridor Visioning, 2014-2015, with Mardi Gras Indian Council, The Painia Family, Milne Inspiration Center, Harmony Neighborhood Redevelopment, Restaurant Opportunities Center, Boutique Hotel Group, Kuts Unlimited Barbershop, Young Aspirations Young Artists, Felicity Redevelopment, Tulane Regional Urban Design Center, and Louisiana State University's Robert Reich School of Landscape Architecture

Red Beans Roundtables Speaker Series, 2014-2016

Center for Sustainable Engagement and Design Environmental Learning and Research, 2014-2015, with Center for Sustainable Engagement and Design • 5620 Florida Avenue

Sankofa Mobile Market, 2015, with Sankofa CDC • Retired in 2017

Oretha Castle Haley Boulevard: Past Present Future Exhibit, 2015, with Clio Associates and New Orleans Redevelopment Authority

Guide to Street Performance in the French Quarter and Marigny Advocacy Publication, 2015, with Music & Culture Coalition of New Orleans

Camp City Park Visioning, 2015, with City Park New Orleans, Ashe Cultural Arts Center Kuumba Institute, and The Net Charter High School Summer Design/Construction Class

APEX Youth Center Outdoor Space Visioning, 2015, with APEX Youth Center

Vision House Visioning, 2015-2016, with Women with a Vision

Urban Orders Collaborative Conference, 2017, with Aarhus University, Denmark

The Cost of Home Exhibit, 2016–2017, with This Creative Lab

Rental Conditions Advocacy Campaign, 2016, with Greater New Orleans Fair Housing Action Center

Housing NOLA Advocacy Campaign, 2016, with Greater New Orleans Housing Alliance

Ozanam Inn Dayspace, 2016, with Ozanam Inn • Demolished 2019

Locating **New Orleans: An Exploration on Shaky Ground** Exhibit, 2016, with New Orleans Center for Creative Arts

LEAD Study Advocacy Campaign, 2016, with New Orleans Lead Exposure Assessment for Drinking Water Project at Louisiana State University Health Sciences Center

Edible Schoolyard Outdoor Classroom Visioning, 2016-2017, with First Line Schools, Edible Schoolyard New Orleans, and Phillis Wheatley Community School

Community Book Center Interior Renovation, 2016, with Community Book Center • 2523 Bayou Road

Behavioral Health and Schools Advocacy, 2016, with Recovery School District

Groundwork Solar Bench, 2017, with Groundwork New Orleans Green Team

Gander Point, 2017, with City Park New Orleans • 30 Magnolia Drive

Big Class Writers Room, 2017, with Sylvanie Williams College Prep • Demolished 2018

Healthy Tremé Housing Research, 2017, with Blue Cross & Blue Shield Louisiana, Tulane University Partnership for Healthcare Innovation, and Greater Treme Consortium

RUBARB Entry Porch, 2018, with Rusted Up Beyond All Recognition Community Bike Shop • 2239 Piety Street

Terrytown Planning Study, 2018 - 2019, with Terrytown Civic Association, Jefferson Parish Economic Development Commission, New Orleans Metropolitan Association of Realtors, and Home Builders Association of Greater New Orleans

Undesign the Redline Exhibit, 2018, with Designing the WE

Jane Place 223 Warehouse Visioning, 2017-2018, with Jane Place Neighborhood Sustainability Initiative

International High School Renovation Visioning, 2019, with International High School New Orleans

Groundwork Earth Lab, 2018, with Groundwork and The Green Team • 1027 Spain Street

Resurrection After Exoneration Visioning, 2019, with Resurrection After Exoneration

Hotel Hope Hexscape, 2019, with Hotel Hope • Private Location

Farmacia, 2019, with NewCorp Inc. • 1831-1835 Old Roman Street

Bayou Sauvage Pavilion and Birding Outlook, 2019, with Bayou Sauvage National Wildlife Refuge • Not Constructed at Bayou Sauvage; Alternate, Private Location

Apothecarts, 2020, with Solitary Gardens and Resurrection After Exoneration

Water Isn't a Game Exhibit, 2020, with The Water Collaborative

Covenant House Care Center Lobby Visioning, 2021–2022, with Covenant House New Orleans 611 N. Rampart Street

Sugar Roots Farm Outdoor Classroom Pavilion, 2021-2022, with Sugar Roots Farm • 10701 Willow Drive

Legacy of Central City Exhibit, 2022, with Civic Studio

STEM Library Lab, 2022-2023, with STEM Library Lab • 3011 N I 10 Service Rd E, Metairie

Monroe Louisiana Connectivity Planning Study, 2022-2023, with the City of Monroe, LA

Extractivism Exhibit, 2023, with Anya Groner & Jazmin Miller

Broad Street Corridor Planning Study, 2023-2024, with Broad Community Connections

Play It Louder Exhibit, 2023, with Solitary Gardens and the John Thompson Legacy Center

Materials of Abolition Installations, & John Thompson Legacy Center Visioning, 2023, with Solitary Gardens • 1212 St. Bernard Avenue

Sprout Pavilion, 2024, with Sprout NOLA • 2510 Lafitte Avenue

What Matters Here?!. Exhibit, 2024-2025, with Tulane Landscape Architecture & Engineering

Small Center Staff

Current Team Members

Ann Yoachim, Director (2018 - present)
Emilie Taylor Welty, Assistant Director, Design/Build (2006 - present)
Nick Jenisch, Assistant Director, Urban Design (2013 - present)
Brandon Surtain, Assistant Director, Community Engagement (2024 - present)
Ben Derlan, Project Manager (2024 - present)
Amy Lenkiewicz, AmeriCorps VISTA (2025 - present)

Past Team Members

Alan Lewis, Founding Director (2005-2006)
Dan Etheridge, Founding Assistant Director (2005-2013)
Scott D. Bernhard, Director (2006-2012)
Olivia Stinson, Senior Program Coordinator (2006)
Alison Popper, Graphic Designer (2009-2010)
Carey Clouse, Project Manager (2011-2012)
Maurice Cox, Director (2012-2014)
Dozenia Marshall, Accountant (2012-2015)
Jenga Mwendo, Engagement Coordinator (2013-2014)
Maggie Hansen, Assistant Director (2014), Director (2015-2017)
John Coyle, AmeriCorps VISTA (2014–2015)
Suzanne-Juliette Mobley, Public Programs Manager (2015-2018)
Donn Peabody, Operations Coordinator (2015-2019)
Shoshana Gordon, AmeriCorps VISTA (2015-2016), Program Assistant (2017-2018)
Rashidah Williams, Assistant Director (2017-2021)
Jose Cotto, Collaborative Design Project Manager (2019- 2024)
Endale Bekele, AmeriCorps VISTA (2023-2024)

Students

Students are critical to the success of every project Small Center completes. Their energy, design skills, and creativity help push each project across the finish line, creating lasting impact across New Orleans. To the extent possible, students in design-build classes, Small Center seminars, project interns, Graduate Research Fellows, and Public Interest Design Fellows (*) are listed below by year of participation. More comprehensive information is archived at the website: small.tulane.edu

2005 • Jerry Blanchard • Gerren Clark • Jeff Gow • Jon Hagar • Jess Helbling • Stuart Hubner • Matt Hux • Carol Knight • Jackie Petterson • Emilie Taylor • Blythe Woodward • Jennifer Good Zurik

2006 • Tim Adams Jr. • Sam Applebaum • Alan Bell • Rebecca Bortolin • Jared Bowers • Ned Brown • Emily Brudenell • Lauren Butz • Claire Cahan • Vincent Cangiamilla • Rob Cogliandro • Kristyn Cosgrove • Nick Crowley • Robert Deacon • David Demsey • Erika Edgley • Mark Enlow • Jordan Gargas • Greg Hayslett • Jason Heinze • Victoria Hernandez • Becky Hutchinson • Tyler Hutcherson • Matt Hux • Maggie Joyce • Julie Kaminski • Mike Kazanzis • Sean Kirkland • Joseph Lai • Emily Levings • Charles Lucia • Andrea Martin • Nicole McGlinn • Trevor Meeks • David Merlin • Reade Nossoman • Miji Park • Craig Parker • Andrea Patrick • Adam Porter • Jonathan Reyes • Carlos Sanchez • Matt Shaver • Kristine Shull • David Siegel • Heather Skeehan • Daren Sodowski • Ashley Sparks • Diana Steig • Emilie Taylor • Art Terry • Steve Thesman • Francisco Tirado • Maggie Van Dusen • Sam Vasquez • Ben Wasserman • Jared Watson • Seth Welty • Carl Westerman • Daniel Zangara • Jesse Zryb

2007 • Tim Adams Jr. • Christina Alvarado-Suarez • Alan Bell • Rebecca Bortolin • Emily Brudenell •Lauren Butz • Adriana Camacho • Vincent Cangiamilla • Rob Cogliandro • Kristyn Cosgrove • Nick Crowley • Ian Daniels • Amarit Dulyapaibul • Maggie Van Dusen • Erika Edgley • Jordan Gargas • Nik Haak • Chris Halbrooks • Greg Hayslett • Jason Heinze • Victoria Hernandez • Cassandra Howard • Tyler Hutcherson • Joseph Lai • Emily Levings • Kimberly Lewis • Caroline Lossack • Charles Lucia • Mike Kazanzis • Sean Kirkland • Nicole Magnellia • Alex Mangimelli • Andrea Martin • Eric McClam • Trevor Meeks • David Merlin • Scott Mucci • Reade Nossoman • Miji Park • Craig Parker • Adam Porter • Jonathan Reyes • Casey Roccanova • Amanda Rosen • Carter Scott • Matt Shaver • Kristine Shull • David Siegel • Steve Smith • Daren Sadowsky • Ashley Sparks • Lori Storm • Diana Steig • Francisco Tirado • Sam Vasquez • Ben Wasserman • Jared Watson • Seth Welty • Carl Westerman • Daniel Zangara • Jesse Zryb

2008 Christina Alvarado-Suarez • Robert Baddour • Alan Bell • Amanda Brendle • Monica

Breziner • Adriana Camacho • Nick Cecchi • Katie Champagne • Nick Chan • Chad Cramer • Ian Daniels • Susan N. Danielson • David Demsey • David Dieckhoff • Amarit Dulyapaibul • Shannon Farrell • Ben Flatau • Matt Fox • Kevin Garfield • Lauren Goetz • Royce Evan Gracey • Corey Green • Nik Haak • Chris Halbrooks • Meaghan Hartney • Greg Hayslett • Matthew Hostetler • Cassandra Howard • Helen Jeurgens • Michael Keller • Colm M. Kennedy • Joseph Keppel • Peter Kilgust • Zach Lamb • Kimberly Lewis • Caroline Lossack • Nicole Magnellia • Nicolas Mallet • Alex Mangimelli • Lauren Martino • Eric McClam • Suzanne Monaco • Scott Mucci • Alex Nassar • Emily Orgeron • JP Pacelli • Miji Park • Alison Popper • Marian Prado • Luis Quinones • Marie Richard • Cameron Ringness • Casey Roccanova • Amanda Rosen • Sarah Satterlee • Gregor Schuller • Carter Scott • Steve Smith • Lori Storm • Emilie Taylor • Art Terry • Kevin Tully • Karla Valdivia • Colin VanWingen • Ben Wasserman • Carl Westerman • Bliss Young

2009 • Danielle Abelow • Ryan Anderson • Robert Baddour • Greg Barton • Michael Battipaglia • Scott Berger • Thomas J Bogan • Will Bradshaw • Amanda Brendle • Monica Breziner • Adriana Camacho • Nick Cecchi • Katie Champagne • Nick Chan • Michael Cohen • Chad Cramer • Susan N. Danielson • Amarit Dulyapaibul • Shannon Farrell • Ben Flatau • Matt Fox • Kevin Garfield • Jennifer Gaugler • Lauren Goetz • Zachary Gong • Royce Evan Gracey • Corey Green • Chris Halbrooks • Meghan Hartney • Matthew Hostetler • Whitney Huver • Garrett Jacobs • Helen Jeurgens • Ana Jimenez • Dan Kautz • Michael Keller • Colm M. Kennedy • Joseph Keppel • Peter Kilgust • Jason Liu • Nicolas Mallet • Lauren Martino • Frederica Merkel • Scott Mikawa • Rebecca Miller • Kristian Mizes • Suzanne Monaco • Alex Nassar • Ian O'Cain • Emily Orgeron • JP Pacelli Allison Popper • Marian Prado • Luis Quinones • Marie Richard • Sarah Rinehart • Gregor Schuller • Dorothy Shepard • Art Terry • Kevin Tully • Karla Valdivia • Colin VanWingen • Bliss Young

2010 • Danielle Abelow • Cristina Alvarado • Evan Amato • Ryan Anderson • Mira Asher • Zin Min Aye • Stephen Baker • James Ball • Michael Battipaglia • Scott Berger • Alexandra Bojarski-Stauffer • Will Bradshaw • Mary Catherine Bullock • Scott Burroughs • Jarelle Carriere • Michelle Carroll • Laura Casaccio • Hee Cho • Michael Cohen • Veronica Cordova • Sophie Dardant • Elizabeth Davis • Matt Decotiis • Daniel Demeules • Alyce Deshotels • Natan Diacon-Furtado • Laura DiIorio • John Dwyerv Nels Erickson • Ben Flatau • Rachel Finkelstein • Sean Fisher • Matt Fox • Patrick Franke • Joshua Frederick • Jennifer Gaugler • Cassandra Gibbs • Zachary Gong • Marianne Graffam • Andrew Graham • Seneca Gray • Corey Green • Ellen Hailey • Meghan Hartney • Katie Healey • Jared Heuter • Natalia Hidalgo • Whitney Huver • Garrett Jacobs • Helen Jeurgens • Jade Jiambutr • Ana Jimenez • Ross Kelley • Colm Kennedy • Ryan Keszczyk • Lindsey Kiefer • Alissa Kingsley • Mike Landry • Jake Lazere • Emile Lejeune • Vicky Leung • Sam Levin • Jason Levy • Xiaoyun Li • Jason Liu • Marda Lugar • Mary Beth Luster • Jeremy Machicek • Jeremy Maloney • Lauren Martino • Jordan Matthews • Andrew Mayronne • Frederica Merkel • Scott Mikawa • Rebecca Miller

• Oren Mitzner • Kathy Mu • Kevin Muni • Mike Murray • John Nelson • Samantha Nourse • Ian O'Cain • Jess O'Dell • Ellanny Page • Justin Park • Robert Pekara • Fernando Polo • Allison Powell • Marian Prado • Devon Reynolds • Sarah Rinehart • J. Cameron Ringness • Alison Rodberg • Brad Rohman • Nicholas Sackos • Julie Sanders • Sarah Satterlee • Allison Schiller • Dorothy Shepard • Justin Siragusa • Lori Storm • Brian Sulley • Eric Sullivan • Christopher Tellone • Ana Lucia Teran • Art Terry • William Trakas • Claire Tritschler • Lorrie Tumlinson • Karla Valdivia • Erin Vaughn • Michael Visintainer • Michael Welsh • Jen Wickham • Nichole Woggon

2011 • Evan Amato • Mira Asher • Zin Min Aye • Steven Baker • Michael Battipaglia • Scott Berger • Alexandra Bojarski-Stauffer • Will Bradshaw • Jerelle Carriere • Michelle Carroll • Mary Catherine Bullock • Hee Cho • Michael Cohen • Sophie Dardant • Matt Decotiis • Alyce Deshotels • Natan Diacon-Furtado • John Dwyer • Nels Erickson • Rachel Finkelstein • Sean Fisher • Patrick Franke • *Cassandra Gibbs (Sizeler Fellow) • Zachary Gong • Marianne Graffam • Seneca Gray • Frances Guevara • Ellen Hailey • Katie Healey • Natalia Hidalgo • Helen Jeurgens • Jade Jiambutar • Lindsey Kiefer • Alyssa Kingsley • Mike Landry • Jake Lazere • Emile Lejeune • Vicky Leung • Sam Levin • Jason Levy • Xiaoyun Li • Marda Lugar • Mary Beth Luster • Jeremy Maloney • Jordan Matthews • Andrew Mayronne • Scott Mikawa • Rebecca Miller • Oren Mitzner • Kathy Mu • Kevin Muni • John Nelson • Ian O'Cain • Jess O'Dell • Ellanny Page • Justin Park • Robert Pekara • Fernando Polo • Allison Powell • Cameron Ringness • Alison Rodberg • Brad Rohman • Nicholas Sackos • Julie Sanders • Sarah Satterlee • Allison Schiller • Dorothy Shepard • Justin Siragusa • Brian Sulley • Christopher Tellone • Ana Lucia Teran • Art Terry • William Trakas • Claire Tritschler • Erin Vaughn • Michael Welsh • Jen Wickham • Nichole Woggon

2012 • Evan Amato • Mira Asher • Zin Min Aye • Steven Baker • Scott Berger • Victoria Bryant • Hee Cho • Jose Cotto • Sophie Dardant • Matt Decotiis • Katherine DeLacy • *Natan Diacon-Furtado (Sizeler Fellow) • Hunter Duplantier • Gage Edwards • Rachel Finkelstein • Sean Fisher • Rena Foster • Patrick Franke • Marianne Graffam • Seneca Gray • Emily Green • Ellen Hailey • Katie Healey • Natalia Hidalgo • Charlotte Hutton • Bahareh Javadi • Jade Jiambutar • Whitney Jordan • Leslie Katz • Lindsey Kiefer • Michael Kirschner • Sarah Knapp • Mike Landry • Emile LeJeune • Vicky Leung • Sam Levin • Jason Levy • Marda Lugar • Mary Beth Luster • Jeremy Maloney • Andrew Mayronne • Jacob McGregor • Kevin Michniok • Rebecca Miller • Oren Mitzner • *Evan Morris • Kevin Muni • Danielle Musselman • John Nelson • Ian O'Cain • Ellanny Page • Justin Park • Robert Pekara • Fernando Polo • Allison Powell • Cameron Ringness • Alison Rodberg • Brad Rohman • Nicholas Sackos • Julie Sanders • Allison Schiller • Risa Schoenfeld • Justin Siragusa • Brian Sulley • Christopher Tellone • Ana Lucia Teran • William Trakas • Claire Tritschler • Erin Vaughn • Guan Wang • Michael Welsh

2013 • Dan Akerley • Madison Baker • Steven Baker • Michael Battipaglia • Vincent Baudoin

• Casey Bemis • Victoria Bryant • Michelle Carroll • Michael Cohen • Joseph A. Colon • Sara Conner • Rachel Conques • Ruben Contreras • Lee Cooper • *Jose Cotto • John Coyle • Sarah Cumming • Katherine Delacey • *Daisy Dodge • Hunter Duplantier • Maggie Easley • Gage Edwards • Carly Epler • Michelle Finan • Rena Foster • Zachary Gong • Kyle Graham • Emily Green • Elisha Grossman • Annelise Haskell • Ellen Hearle • *Elizabeth Himmel • Charlotte Hutton • *Emma Jasinski • Bahareh Javadi • Tara Jean • Whitney Jordan • Leslie Katz • Michael Kirschner • Sarah Knapp • Kristen Korndoefer • James Lacroix • Katlyn Leach • Logan Leggett • Colleen Loughlin • Kate Luxner • Derek Magee • Gregory Mathieu • Jacob McGregor • Stephanie Mears • Kevin Michniok • Scott Mikawa • Kristian Mizes • Tatyana Moraczewski • Paul Morin • Robert Mosby • Kathy Mu • Danielle Musselman • Sam Naylor • William Nemitoff • Matt Ngo • Ian O'Cain • *Jessica O'Dell • Caitlin Parker • Allison Price • Ali Rex • Devin Reynolds • Ashley Ricketson • Laura Robin • Alison Rodberg • Ian Rosenfield • Kyle Ryan • *Sarah Satterlee • Risa Schoenfeld • Sanaa Shaikh • Jonathan Sharp • *Dorothy Shepard (Sizeler Fellow) • Guan Wang • Gavin West • Alfia White • Grant Whittaker • Fan Xiong • Emily Youngblood • Meredith Zelenka • William Zink

2014 • Katherine Allen • Michael Battipaglia • *Vincent Baudoin • Braham Berg • Hillary Bocash • Rachel Boynton • Michelle Brenner • Kayleigh Bruentrup • Michelle Carroll • Matthew Cerick • Michael Cohen • Victoria Cohen • *Joseph Colón (Sizeler Fellow) • Sara Conner • Ruben Contreras • Lee Cooper • John Coyle • Alisha Croft • Carly Epler • Zachary Gong • Kyle Graham • Peter Henseler • Elizabeth (Lizzie) Himmel • Tanya Hockney • Kelsey Howard • *Stuart Hurt • Emma Jasinkski • Tara Jean • *Jenny Renn Key • Matthew Lamm • Jake Lazere • Colleen Loughlin • Stephanie Mears • *Scott Mikawa • Kossen Miller • Kristian Mizes • Tatyana Moraczewski • Paul Morin • Robert Mosby • Kathy Mu • Danielle Musselman • *Sam Naylor • Matt Ngo • Ian O'Cain • Caitlin Parker • Rosemary Phillips • Olivia Pontiff • *Allison Price • Ali Rex • Ashley Ricketson • Ian Rosenfield • Sanaa Shaikh • Jonathan Sharp • Dorothy Shepard • Kathleen Smith • Heather Tischler • Gavin West • *Alfia White • Grant Whittaker • Emily Youngblood

2015 • Megan Van Artsdalen • Marielle Asenjo • Andrew Balfe • James Ball • Calla Bardwell • Michael Battipaglia • Vince Baudoin • Braham Berg • Abby Bray • Michelle Brenner • Matthew Cerick • Michael Cohen • Joseph A. Colon • Sara Conner • Ruben Contreras • Lee Cooper • John Coyle • Alisha Croft • Luna Eaton • Carly Epler • Lolade Frankel • *Lindsay Girardeau (Sizeler Fellow) • Zachary Gong • Zoe Grosshandler • Peter Henseler • Alec Herskowitz • Elizabeth (Lizzie) Himmel • Emma Jasinkski • Tara Jean • Jenny Renn Key • Logan Leggett • Colleen Loughlin • Eric Lynn • Kyle Maer • Stephanie Mears • Michael Meline • Scott Mikawa • Shelby Mills • Tatyana Moraczewski • Sarah Morasso • Gianna Morelli • Paul Morin • Samuel Naylor • Joseph Newman • Matt Ngo • Catherine Nguyen • Ian O'Cain • Caitlin Parker • Rosemary Phillips • Olivia Pontiff • Allison Price • Ali Rex • *Ashley Ricketson • *Gustavo Rodas • Ian Rosenfield • *John (JD) Scott • Sanaa Shaikh • Jonathan Sharp • Dorothy Shepard

• Kathleen Smith • Laura Stokley • *Lauren Taylor • Melinda Telford • Seth Voiron • Alfia White • Grant Whittaker • Emily Youngblood

2016 • Jeremiah Anyaele • Hannah Bahney • Gabby Black • Chistophe Blanchard • Abby Bray • Ian Carr • *Shirley Chen • Jordan Conway • Rebecca Cumming • *Katarina Dvorak • Luna Eaton • Dana Elliot • Clifford Fox • Alex Goessler • *Javier Gonzalez • Sara Allen Harper • Kristen Hill • Jonathan House • *Pavlo Iosipiv • Maggie Lloyd • Haley Lindsley • Christopher Longman • *John Ludlam • Kyle Maer • *Chesley McCarty •Kristen McDaniel • Wells Megalli • Rachel Neue Matt Raybon • *Cassidy Rosen • Cassidy Self • Ethan Shaw • Fernanda Silva • Me'osha Solsberry • Lauren Taylor • Jill Thompson • Camly Tram • Ben Tulman • *Evan Wagner (Sizeler Fellow) • Alex Walker • Brian Webber • Lei Ying

2017 • Abdulrahman Alharbi • Ahmed Alhumaid • Paula Bechara • Camille Bernsten • Dia Biagioni •Abby Bray • Antonia Butwell • Courtney Castleman • Monica Marrero Ciuro • Blaise Courtney • R. Chris Daemmrich • X Daminos • Joseph D'Arco • *Kekeli Dawes (Eskew+Dumez+Ripple Fellow) • Keristen Edwards • Dana Elliot • Allison Gerstley • Andrew Glassman • Carson Hall • Paul Holmes • *Carolyn Isaacson • Laruschka Joubert • Bruna Aoki Gandur Khaled • Liu Junyang • Casey Last • Izabela Lotozo • Kyle Maer • Magda Magierski • David Maples • *Christie Melgar • Shelby Mitchinson • Katelyn Morgan • Rachel Neue • Bansi Patel • Isaura Perez • Elliott Petterson • Rachel Rockford • *Ana Laura Sandoval (Adjmi Fellow) • Nicole Saville • Arielle Scher • Annika Schneider • Diego Schubb • *Ryan Shaaban • Ethan Shaw • tephanie Sirhal • Me'osha Solsberry • Sami Tobin • Camly Tram • Julian Tricamo-Palmer • Ben Tulman • Evan Wagner • *Kelsey Willis (Sizeler Fellow) • Jesse Williams • Wei Xiao • Kairui Zhang • Na Zhao

2018 • Abigail Allshouse • Zachary Banks • Michelle Barrett • Madison Beck • Leta Berkowitz • Elisa Bernstein • Andres Hartman Blau • Abby Boedigheimer • Madeleine Capozzoli • Courtney Castleman • Allison Conn • Kay M. Curtis • Alyson Demskie • *Dana Elliot • Jacqueline Esmay • Jared L. Faske • Dylan R. Goldweit-Denton • *Seneca Gray (Eskew+Dumez+Ripple Fellow) • *Clayton Hakes (Sizeler Fellow) • Carolyn Isaacson • Emily M. Kanner • Kate Katz • Bryn E. Koeppel • Andras Kozicz • Bruna Aoki Gandur Khaled • Riley V. Lacalli • Caroline H. LaFleche • Casey Last • Ming Lin • Junyang Liu • Linlu Liu • Kristen McDaniel • *Collin Moosbrugger (Adjmi Fellow) • Katelin Morgan • Ana Rebeca Chu Noriega • Emma Olson • Erica Perine • Sarah Rivard • Jessica Roy • Olivia Sahai • *Lucy Satzewich • Brandon Surtain • Margaret H. Swinford • Isabella Zannier Trejo • John Tufts • Max Warshaw

2019 • *Hannah Bannister (Sizeler Fellow) • *Abby R. Boedigheimer • Luke Borden • Courtney Castleman • Paolo Cattani • Madison C. Cook • *Griffin Daly • Jordan Day • Dana Elliot • Joanne Engelhard • Jacqueline Esmay • Maria Espinoza • Perry M. Feinstein • Bradley Friedman • Clayton Haykes • Austin Hogans • Caroline LaFleche • Tao Li • Ming Lin • Collin Moosbrugger • Katelin Morgan • Kyra Nasser • *Chewys Parra-Paulino (Adjmi Fellow) • Gabrielle R. Proeh • Shanelle Reese • James Rennert • Michelle Sandquist • *Taylor

Scott • Jacob J. Smiley • Brandon Surtain • *Maddison Wells (Eskew+Dumez+Ripple Fellow) • Lingfeng Ye • Caroline F. Zimmermann

2020 • Elizabeth Bateman • Jeremy Baudy • Kayla Buffington • Cece Callwood • *Anne Davis • Anna Deeg • Claire Divito • Rebecca Dunn • Adrian Evans • Bianca Falanga • Kalyn Faller • Jake Hesse • Michael Heitz • Xiaolan Lan • Erik Luthringhausen • Danelle Martin • *Emi Morita • Will Neild • Chewys Parra Paulino • Andrew Porten • Ben Racusin • Shanelle N. Reese • Noam Saul • Danielle Scheeringa • Walid Shahin • Bhumika Shirole • Zach Speroni • *Gabrielle Rashleigh • *James Rennert • Dana Ridenour • Evan Warder

2021 • Merrie Afseth • Brianna Baldwin • Le'Bryant Bell • *Zachary Braaten • Griffin Daly • Sophia Del Sole • *Kelsie Donovan • Kareem Elsandouby • Luke Escobar • *Melanie Evans • Ellen Feringa • *Olivia Foster • Geoff Gibbons • Nick George • Brandon Israel • Ella Jacobs • *Seth Laskin • *Samantha Lindley • Connor Little • Mandii Malhotra • Valentina Mancera • Johnathan Michka • Sofia Perrotta • Mensi Malina Pickard • James Poche • Natalie Rendleman • David Rodriguez • Katie Schultz • Karan Sharma • Bruno Soria • Giuliana Vaccarino Gearty • Yao Zhang

2022 • Rachel Abrahams • Brianna Baldwin • Rachel Bennett • Ben Brimer • Belinda Chau • Charles Crawford • Katherine Dunn • Chelsea Kilgore • Miya Kutchins • Zirui Liao • Lauren Liroff • Katarina Luehrsen • Charley Polaner • Talia Pomp • Sarah Quinn • Karan Sharma • Riley Siltler • Delaney Smith • Sam Spencer • Frank Taylor • William Trotter • Giuliana Vaccarino Gearty • Josiah Ramirez • Maria Arrieta Vallarino • Jose Varela Castillo • Antonia Villafranca • Bryce Winter • Chenbo Xing • Yao Zhang • Esther Zulem

2023 • Margot Barberich • Malia Bavuso • Anna Kathryn Becker • *Emily Brandt • Shanelle Brown • Abby Carlton • Tahlor Cleveland • Susan Critchfield • Elka Cuttino • *Analiese DeSaw • Nicole Feig • Sarah Fisher • Anthony Gagliano • Kate Galvin • Natalia Guerrero • *Kristin Hamilton • Aubrey Hash • Rin Hu • Tracy Jones • Grant Jorissen • An Le • Tyler Levitt • Paolo Wong Man • Erin Matsuoka • Joshua McGrew • Brooke Mehney • Marhaba Nigar • Tom O'Brien • Ryan Russell • Katherine Schwab • Allison Slomski • Naomi Smith • Riley Siltler • Elliot Slovis • Joey Tomshe • Yi Wei

2024 • *Corwin Almo • Rose Barnes • Ruby Bienen • *Emilia Bertoli • Lindsay Bopp • Livi Bowers • Emily Brandt • Shanelle Brown • Alex Cohen • *Ben Cornett • Lily Cummings • Bella Davies • Grace DeLaune • Analiese DeSaw • Charlotte Fisher • Madison Grenauer • Chester Griffiths • Brian Harris • Bobby Hess • Charlotte Kelley • Jane Lee • Jack Levine • Sophia Lindahl • Emma Lindley • Charlotte Love • Kayleigh Macumber • Emily Morris • Paul Onu • Clara Quandt • Katherine Schwab • Cole Schwabacher • Madeline Shade • Riley Siltler • *Kris Smith • Jackson Stephens • *Emmet Tanzer-Tragatsch • Alexa Trapani • Jose Varela Castillo • *Sofia Vladimir • Daphne Vorel • Josh Warsaw • Walter Workman

Contributor Biographies

Maggie Hansen is an Assistant Professor in Landscape Architecture at the University of Texas at Austin. Her research, teaching, and creative work draw from theater, gardening, participatory art, and activist methods to recover design as a relational practice. From 2014-17, she was Director of the Albert and Tina Small Center for Collaborative Design and she continues to write, teach, and research models of participatory practice across disciplines. She is co-curator of *Ditched Schemes*, a zine and podcast that explores unrealized projects, creative risk-taking, and notions of success in design.

Nick Jenisch is Associate Director of Urban Design at the Albert and Tina Small Center for Collaborative Design and a Lecturer at Tulane School of Architecture and Built Environment. He has been engaged in public interest design for twenty years, with projects encompassing architectural design-build, water management, park & public open space design, and cultural sustainability. Though focused on local planning, policy, and design implementation, he has also directed multiple international regional planning and urban design projects. He utilizes engaged planning and design processes to educate, identify needs and priorities of partner organizations, spur collaborative action, and influence policy decisions. Working to address the larger issues facing our city, his research focuses on neighborhood stability through urban density, affordable housing, schools, and health.

Ann Yoachim is the Director of the Albert and Tina Small Center for Collaborative Design and Professor of Practice at Tulane School of Architecture and Built Environment. She has a twenty-five-year-long career of working at the intersection of people, environment and health. Much of this work has focused on building relationships between organizations, institutions, individuals, and disciplines to effect change. Ann holds a Master of Public Health from Tulane University and a bachelor's degree in environmental studies and political science from Dickinson College. From 2012-2013, she was a Loeb Fellow at the Harvard Graduate School of Design.

Emilie Taylor Welty is a licensed architect and a leader in design-build education whose research and practice are grounded in material explorations and expanding access to design. She is an Associate Professor at Tulane School of Architecture and Built Environment, where she also serves as the Architecture Program Director. At Tulane, Taylor Welty has led over thirty applied research projects through Small Center, including internationally recognized projects such as Grow Dat Youth Farm, Sugar Roots, and the Apothecarts. Emilie's work is published in a range of academic journals and has been recognized for excellence internationally and nationally, including by the AIA/ACSA Practice and Leadership award. Emilie is also co-founder of Colectivo, a New Orleans-based architecture firm.

Anna Livia Brand, PhD., works at the intersection of race and space, specifically looking at historic Black mecca neighborhoods and how they change through processes of redevelopment and resistance. Brand is interested in everyday landscapes and built environments, from the materiality and local geography that supports and sustains us to the ways that people shape and create a place for themselves, including the ways that that people are imagining more socially just places and communities. She has worked professionally as both a planner and designer. Brand is an Associate Professor of Landscape Architecture at UC Berkeley.

Austin Allen, Ph.D., is an Associate Professor of Practice at the University of Texas at Arlington's School of Architecture. A frequent design collaborator on Small Center projects, Allen's interests lie in resilience, recovery, and regeneration of landscapes and places, urbanism, public space, and public media, including film studies.

Scott Bernhard is the Jean and Saul A. Mintz Associate Professor at Tulane School of Architecture and Built Environment in New Orleans, where he has been a member of the faculty for more than twenty-six years. As Director of Small Center from 2007-12, Scott was instrumental in establishing the program as Tulane School of Architecture's primary venue for outreach. He was design lead for numerous projects, including Grow Dat Youth Farm. Scott continues to be an important ally and advisor to Small Center's team, and a persuasive voice in advocating for architectural service learning.

Jackson Blalock connected with Small Center while rebuilding in the Hollygrove neighborhood after Hurricane Katrina. He was one of the co-founders of Transitional Spaces and Parisite DIY Skatepark and worked with Small Center on several other projects. Today, Jackson manages Pacific Conservation District's Marine + Estuarine Resilience Program, which assists southwest Washington State's rural coastal communities to adapt to ecological changes, such as sea level rise, erosion, and habitat shifts. His work continues to use collaborative processes influenced by Small Center's methods. He has a background in construction, architecture (BA, Clemson University), and landscape architecture (MLA, University of Washington).

Pam Broom is a dedicated nonprofit administration professional specializing in project planning, implementation, evaluation, research, and grant writing. As a community development consultant, she specializes in urban agriculture, green infrastructure, and intergenerational connectedness. Her work centers on promoting "food as medicine" through infrastructure planning and hands-on growing initiatives. A Tulane University graduate who completed advanced studies in Urban Anthropology at the University of New Orleans, Pam brings a deeply informed perspective to her work. She is a frequent advisor to Small Center, where she champions projects that empower communities through collaborative design and sustainable practices.

Max Ciardullo served as the Policy Analyst and then Director of Policy and Communications at Louisiana Fair Housing Action Center (LaFHAC) from 2014-2023. He now works as the Director of Research for the Redress Movement, a national nonprofit focused on redressing the harms of segregation.

Maurice Cox served as Director of Small Center from 2012-14. He went on to serve as Director of Planning and Development for the City of Detroit between 2015-2019 and Commissioner of Planning and Development for the City of Chicago between 2019-2023, where he focused on the adaptive challenges facing contemporary urban revitalization.

Dan Etheridge co-founded Small Center and served as Assistant Director from 2005-13. A skilled connector, he went on to co-found and direct the Design Futures Student Leadership Forum, a program that built a network of design and planning schools across America. He recently returned to Australia where he is Engagement Director of the Living Lab Northern Rivers.

Rashida Ferdinand is the Founder and Chief Executive Officer of Sankofa Community Development Corporation (CDC) in New Orleans, Louisiana. She earned a BFA from Howard University and an MFA from Syracuse University, with a background in the arts, which informs her approach to community revitalization. A fourth-generation resident of the Lower Ninth Ward, Rashida was displaced by Hurricane Katrina for more than two years while her home was reconstructed. In 2008, she founded Sankofa CDC to address public health, environmental restoration, and economic development in underserved communities. Her deep-rooted connection to this community has significantly influenced her dedication to its revitalization and environmental stewardship.

Johanna Gilligan is an entrepreneur, educator, and developer, whose work aims to foster stronger social cohesion and healthier communities. After Hurricane Katrina, Johanna founded Grow Dat Youth Farm, a space for employment, education, and leadership development for young adults. Small Center designed the Grow Dat campus, which is now the largest farm in New Orleans. Johanna is a Loeb Fellow and is currently the Deputy CEO for Homewise, a CDFI and developer that makes homeownership accessible to all in New Mexico.

Anya Groner's award-winning writing explores the changing environment's impact on community and equity. Her journalism and essays are featured in *The New York Times, The Guardian, Orion Magazine* and *The Atlantic*. Her audio reporting and production can be heard on Monument Lab's mini-podcast *Plot of Land* and on WWNO/WRKF's *Sea Change* podcast. Her fiction aims to illuminate historic moments that might otherwise feel unrecognizable to contemporary readers. She's taught storytelling in high schools, colleges, and professional settings, including at public health conferences and to immigration lawyers, and encourages students to pursue their curiosity wherever it may take them.

Doug Harmon served as director of the CITYbuild program, which operated from 2005–2007. Doug led multiple significant Small Center projects, including the Ozanam Inn Day Space, and helped to shape the Center's model of studio instruction. Doug continues to shape the city through his own design and fabrication practice and volunteer work. He is founder and director of Revival Workshop, an apprenticeship program teaching high level woodcraft skills to formerly incarcerated men through the production of fine furniture.

Bahareh Rana Javadi is the Director of Co-Design at Concordia, where she manages projects through all phases of engagement, design, and construction, supports firm operations, and fosters the implementation of co-design throughout Concordia's interdisciplinary practice. Education and youth empowerment are central to Bahareh's practice, and she works to share her passion for collaborative place-making in all of her projects. Bahareh is a Chicago native and credits her love of people-watching and urban life to her hometown and her continued growth as a community-focused designer to her adopted home in New Orleans.

Melissa Lee leads Public Works' urban planning practice, called Community Health, which focuses on creating stronger neighborhoods through planning, placemaking, economic development, and community engagement. While at the New Orleans Redevelopment Authority (2012-18), Melissa launched and managed significant grantmaking initiatives, including Façade RENEW, an award-winning initiative developed in partnership with Small Center.

Jazmin "Jazzy" Miller is a director, actor, playwright, and filmmaker residing in Memphis, TN. Jazzy is also an informed theatre artist and advocate for racial justice and social change. Her most recent project, *Jonesland*, is a documentary film about Black land ownership, survival, and Black ecological legacy in St. James, Louisiana, where her family owns sixty-six acres of land on the Mississippi River. Jazzy has also conducted extensive biographical research on Sojourner Truth and wrote a one-woman play about her life, *Journey of Truth*, which has been performed across the United States, Latin America, Africa, and Asia. Jazzy holds an M.F.A in Theatre Direction from the University of Memphis and a B.A. in Theatre from Rhodes.

Suzanne-Juliette Mobley is the Director of Research at Monument Lab. Her previous work as Advocacy Director at Colloqate Design earned recognition as one of The Architectural League's 2019 Emerging Voices. As Public Programs Manager of Small Center from 2014-18, Sue led the development of events, exhibitions, workshops, and other activities in the Baronne Street storefront space. With a background in political science, anthropology, and sociology, Sue brings a cross-disciplinary approach to framing, developing, and assessing the results of community-based design work.

Andreanecia Morris has devoted her career to creating affordable housing in New Orleans. She was lead organizer for the Greater New Orleans Housing Alliance (GNOHA) and continues to serve as GNOHA's president. The organization's advocacy supported members and partners in developing approximately 88,000 housing opportunities between 2006 and 2015 in New Orleans. She is a frequent collaborator with Small Center and served as project partner for a housing affordability toolkit in 2016.

Sarah Satterlee is Director of Architecture and Site Development with Community First Village, a permanent supportive housing community for the formerly homeless in Austin, TX. A native New Orleanian, she previously worked with design firm Colectivo on many residential and commercial projects, as well as several community-focused design-build projects with Small Center. Sarah holds an M.Arch from Tulane School of Architecture and Built Environment.

jackie sumell is a multidisciplinary artist and abolitionist inspired by the lives of everyday people. Her work has been exhibited extensively throughout the world. A frequent collaborator with Small Center, as an instructor, advisor and community partner, she brings working methods grounded in activism, transformative justice, education, and mindfulness practices.

Matt Williams is an urban planner, landscape designer and development consultant based in Detroit. He previously served in the Mayor's Office as a Senior Economic Advisor on Neighborhood Economic Development at the City of Detroit. He holds a 2023 National Planning Excellence Award from the American Planning Association for his leadership in neighborhood planning. In 2022, he served in the Distinguished Trott Fellowship at Ohio State University, leading a multidisciplinary course, symposium, and exhibition around vacancy strategies for Detroit. He holds a Bachelor of Science in Economics from the University of Pennsylvania and a Masters in Landscape Architecture from Louisiana State University.

Acknowledgements

This book, like all Small Center projects, was a deeply collaborative endeavor, many years in the making. In 2019, Maggie Hansen and Ann Yoachim began talking about a book reflecting on the Center's work. From these conversations, the structure and themes of this book emerged, and a goal was set for its release as a twenty-year retrospective. Maggie and Nick Jenisch authored the text of the book, exchanging ideas, tracking down information, swapping edits, and curating the guest essays.

Many people have also helped to shape the narrative text, in ways that are not typical of a monograph and difficult to capture through traditional author credits. Project texts, describing the scope of work, partnerships, contributors, and outcomes, are drafted following each project, and these served as starting drafts and background for many of the project descriptions in this book. For this writing, we are grateful to Scott Bernhard, Dan Etheridge, Emilie Taylor Welty, Suzanne-Juliette Mobley, and Jose Cotto. Reflection on the Center's process and outcomes has been enriched through multiple rounds of qualitative interviews led by Suzanne-Juliette Mobley (in 2015), and more recently through a program evaluation led by Jeanne Firth and Ann Yoachim (2020). These interviews and documents shaped the book's outline, while Ann's continued support of the project has made it possible. Emilie Taylor Welty and Ann reviewed multiple drafts of the text and helped to clarify it, and Americorps VISTA Amy Lenkiewicz provided eagle-eyed editing.

Additional thanks is due to Jose Cotto for professionally photographing projects and process, and for selecting images and collaborating on the Smallx20 layout. Many of his photographs richly enhance this book. Small Center research fellow Amy Martin designed the initial graphic layouts for the project, working with Jose and Nick. Specific credits for professional photos appear throughout the book, while uncredited photos appear courtesy of Small Center and were taken by many Small Center staff, faculty, and students.

We offer our sincere appreciation for the time, care, and enthusiasm of our guest essayists, who shared diverse reflections on the city and the Center. Thank you for making the time to contribute your perspective. Together, you give a sense of the breadth of voices that have informed the Center's work over the years.

We are grateful for the support of our institutions, the University of Texas School of Architecture and Tulane School of Architecture and Built Environment. At UT-Austin, we would like to thank the Director of the Urban Design Program, Dean Almy, for his generosity and advice. We are also grateful for the encouragement of UT-Austin colleagues: Mirka Benes, Phoebe Lickwar, Bjorn Sletto, Allan Shearer, Miriam Solis, Dean Heather Woofter, and former dean Michelle Addington. At Tulane, we want to thank Dean Iñaki Alday for his ongoing support of Small Center and this project, and recognize generous support from past deans Kenneth Schwartz, Scott Bernhard, and Reed Kroloff. Publication support was provided by the Urban Design Program at the University of Texas at Austin and the Favrot Research Center (Publication) Fund at Tulane School of Architecture and Built Environment.

Our sincere thanks to the Applied Research and Design board and the team at ORO for a smooth publication process. Thanks to the book's project manager, Jake Anderson, for supporting our work and shepherding the project through production.

Small Center's work over the last twenty years would not be possible without support from individual donors, corporate contributions, and philanthropic foundations. The Center is particularly grateful for the endowed gift from Board of Tulane trustee, former Tulane School of Architecture Dean's Advisory Council member, and Tulane alumnus, Albert H. Small, Jr. '79 and his wife, Tina B. Small.

Finally, we are thankful to all the project partners, advisors, students, faculty, administrators, and friends who have contributed to Small Center's work over the years. Each project, in its own way, is inspiring, beautiful, necessary, and only possible through the patient and generous partnership of all who contribute. We are grateful for how these partnerships have reshaped our understanding of the city and of the design fields. Each collaboration inspires hope that a better world can be realized when we work together.